# 501

## Things <u>YOU</u> Should Have Learned About...

## GRAMMAR

**METRO BOOKS**
NEW YORK
An Imprint of Sterling Publishing
387 Part Avenue South
New York, NY 10016

AUTHOR: Sonia Mehta (in association with Quadrum Solutions)
SERIES ART DIRECTOR: Clare Barber
SERIES EDITOR: Helena Caldon
DESIGN & EDITING: Quadrum Solutions
PUBLISHER: James Tavendale

IMAGES courtesy of www.shutterstock.com;
www.istockphoto.com and www.clipart.com

ISBN 978-1-4351-4614-3

For information about custom editions, special
sales, and premium and corporate purchases,
please contact Sterling Special Sales at 800-805-5489
or specialsales@sterlingpublishing.com

Printed in China

10 9 8 7 6 5 4 3 2 1

www.sterlingpublishing.com

# 501

## Things YOU Should Have Learned About...

## GRAMMAR

METRO BOOKS
NEW YORK

# CONTENTS

**7**  Introduction

**8**  The History of English Grammar

**60**  Key Events in the Evolution of Grammar - A Timeline

**68**  Grammar through the Ages

**100**  English Around the World

**116**  Parts of Speech

**150**  Sanskrit and English Grammar - The Connection

**156**  Fun Facts on English Grammar

**172**  Common Howlers

**184**  Grammar vs. the SMS Generation

**194**  Grammar and the Stalwarts

**208**  Linguists - Study of Language and Grammar

**250**  Index

# INTRODUCTION

Do you think English grammar was introduced in the school syllabus just to make your life difficult? If that's the case, you need to get your hands on this book. It may not hold the promise to make your brawl with grammar any easier, but it'll surely make it more interesting. This book reveals that stalwarts like William Shakespeare and Jane Austen too – like you – just hated following "the rules." What did they do? We're not covering all of that in the introduction; you will have to peek in to find out!

This book is not just a hate list of protests and marches against dear Grammar. We also have ample tidbits on the origin of the big and burly list of "what-shoulds" and "what-shouldn'ts" in the English language; facts that we're sure a Grammar enthusiast would swear by.

Apart from all those interesting details, the book also tells you about the amusing origins of words, the fuss surrounding the Short Message Service, or SMS language (and why purists hate it!), what words make it into the Oxford English Dictionary and what happens to those words that don't.

It's time to find out the truth – one that wasn't even mentioned in your Grammar classes – about this subject. Enjoy!

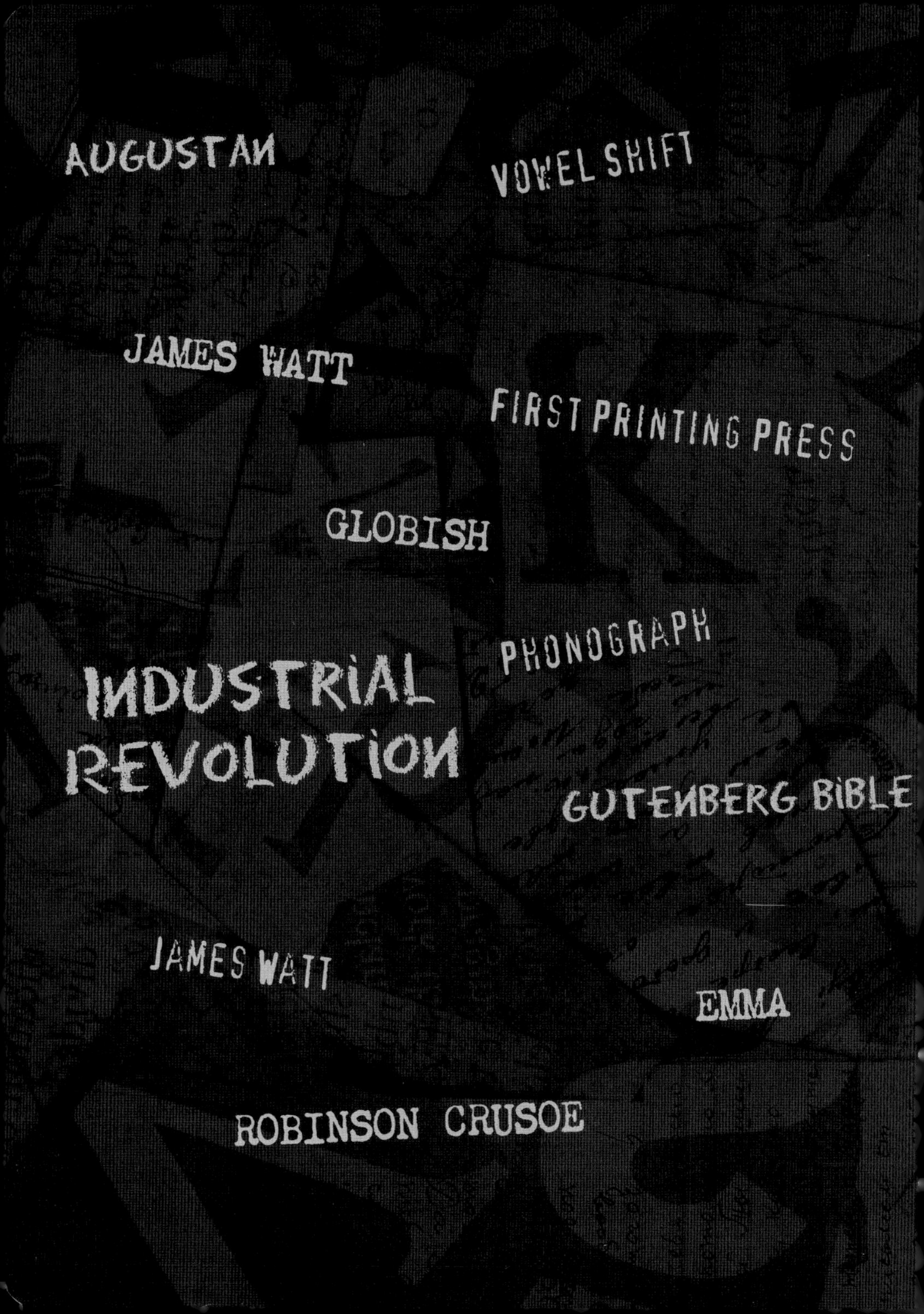

AUGUSTAN

VOWEL SHIFT

JAMES WATT

FIRST PRINTING PRESS

GLOBISH

PHONOGRAPH

INDUSTRIAL
REVOLUTION

GUTENBERG BIBLE

JAMES WATT

EMMA

ROBINSON CRUSOE

SILENT LETTERS

501

VICTORIAN

# The History of English Grammar

ROBINSON
CRUSOE

INDUSTRIAL
REVOLUTION

SUFFRAGE

JAMES WATT

TWAIN

FEMINIST

# RISE OF THE "ENRICHERS" AND THE "PURISTS"

**IN THE YEAR 1417, KING HENRY V** ordered all government documents and private letters to be written in English. This led to the rise of Standard English, which at that time was known as "Chancery English." But English Renaissance truly kicked in only by the middle of 16th century.

## FAST FACT

**📖 THE WRITTEN ENGLISH** used in the official documents at the Court of Chancery, a court of equity in England and Wales, was what set a standard in grammar and vocabulary, and that's where the term "Chancery English" originated.

During this period, a large number of classics were translated into English, and wherever satisfactory English words were not found, they began using terms which were deliberately borrowed from Latin, French or Greek. But then arose a little problem. Some scholars began borrowing and adopting these foreign terms so excessively and mindlessly that it led to one of the first controversies of English language - "The Inkhorn Controversy."

The word "Inkhorn" referred to obscure words. This controversy promptly led to the rise of "The Enrichers" who aimed to enhance the English language with the help of the large European word stock. They were people like Sir Thomas Elyot and Sir Thomas More. Opposed to these scholars were "The Purists," men like Sir John Cheke, who fought to prevent this "foreign attack" on their English and even tried to revive Older English with gallant ventures such as using only Native English words whilst translating the New Testament.

## 3 FAST FACT...

📖 **THE WORD "ENCYCLOPEDIA"** was first defined in Sir Thomas Elyot's Latin dictionary in 1538.

## 4 FAST FACT...

📖 **GREEK SCHOLAR,** Sir John Cheke once said, "I am of this opinion that our own tung should be written cleane and pure, unmixt and unmangeled with borowing of other tunges; wherein if we take not heed by tiim, ever borowing and never paying, she shall be fain to keep her house as bankrupt."

## 5 FAST FACT...

📖 **INKHORN WORDS** "like commit" and "transmit" have survived till today but "demit" was eventually done away with. Similarly, the word "impede" caught on, but "expede" lost out. Why this happened is something nobody can explain.

## 6 FAST FACT...

📖 **PARADISE LOST** is amongst the greatest epics ever written in English. And what makes it even more special is the fact that the author John Milton (who had lost his eyesight by then) would mentally compose the verses at night and in the morning he would dictate them to his aides.

# SILENT LETTERS CREATING CHAOS!

**IN THE EARLY 17TH CENTURY,** people were used to spelling words phonetically, based on the way they sounded, leading to very little uniformity. And just out of respect for the classical languages, the spellings of certain words were slightly tweaked by adding "silent letters," which were written down, but not pronounced.

Take the example of "debt" that first made its way to English in the 1300s as "det" or "dett," as it came from the French word "dete" or "dette," which meant "something owed." Phonologically, this was an apt spelling. But some scholars, who loved fiddling with words, opined that the origin of det or dett shouldn't be French. It should originate from the Latin word "debitum." Sounds classier, doesn't it? And so the necessary changes were made and a "b" got added to det, making it "debt." Same was the case with words like island with a silent "s," and scissor with a "silent" "c."

## FAST FACT...

**THE FIRST ENGLISH GRAMMAR BOOK** "Bref Grammar for English" was published in the year 1586 by Bullokar, and the first English dictionary, "Table Alphabeticall" was produced by Robert Cawdrey in 1604.

## FAST FACT...

**JOHN DRYDEN** was the first person ever known to have worried about the preposition at the end of a sentence.

John Dryden

## 10 THE CONFUSION WITH ADDITIONAL "NOT-SO-SILENT" LETTERS

**IT IS IMPORTANT** to note that while silent letters were being introduced in certain words, in others, additional letters were completely changing the way in which words were being pronounced. Under this category came words such as "perfect and adventure," which were originally "perfet" and "aventure." This led to a large amount of confusion on how the newly spelled words were to be pronounced. Thus, we see that although the spellings of words were being changed to make the chaotic English language more reasonable and logical, it turns out that it only created further mayhem amongst the people.

This was one of the major reasons a number of scholars gained interest in bringing about spelling reform in the 19th century, and thus began regularizing spelling as best they could with the help of tactics such as devising phonetic letters. It was during this time that a number of grammar books and dictionaries were being written and published.

## 11 FAST FACT...

**MATHEMATICIAN JOHN WALLIS** was the first person to study the difference between "shall" and "will" in his publication in the year 1658.

## 12 FAST FACT...

**ROBERT LOWTH'S** "A Short Introduction to English Grammar" published in 1672 was one of the most well-reputed grammar books of its time. A large number of scholars including Noah Webster were believed to borrow from his work. Interesting, isn't it?

# GREAT CONTRIBUTIONS BY THE THOMAS'S AND JOHN'S

**THE PERIOD BETWEEN THE 16TH AND 18TH CENTURY** was called "The Golden Age of English Literature." During this time, English grammar and vocabulary were undergoing great generative activity. Until the 17th century, scholarly works were rarely written in English, as it was believed that the language did not possess the grace and precision of the classical languages.

It was men like Sir Thomas More who first began translating their major works from Latin and French to English. This led to the use of English in literature. Sir Thomas Elyot is another noted English author, philosopher, and lexicographer, who was determined to "augment our Englysshe tongue." His book "Governour," which was about how gentlemen's sons should be brought up, was the first book that stressed on the importance of education in English. Others who left a huge mark in the literary field were Thomas Wyatt and Thomas Champion.

Even so, while we thank the Thomases, let's not forget the Johns because there were also a great number of Johns who dominated the literary field back then. John Donne was largely considered to be the most epic love poet in the English language, and was also well-known for his treatises, sermons, and religious verses in the 17th century. John Webster, and of course, John Milton also made notable contributions to English grammar and literature.

## FAST FACT...

**ENGLISH HISTORIOGRAPHY'S** first masterpiece was Thomas More's "History of King Richard" III which was written in both Latin and English between the years 1513-1518.

## FAST FACT...

**JOHN DONNE** is actually related to Sir Thomas More as his mother is believed to be More's direct descendant.

John Milton

# THE LONE WILLIAM AND HIS MANY "VAGABONDS!"

**IN THE WORDS** of Ben Johnson, Shakespeare "was not of an age, but for all time." That's because Shakespeare made use of the flexible nature of the English language and its grammar rules. He penned down plays and poems that have withstood the test of time, and till today are considered the greatest literary works to have ever been written. He also introduced countless phrases which are commonly used even today, such as "laughing stock," "a foregone conclusion," etc.

William Shakespeare

His ability to be witty, his subtle sarcasm, and his ability to shift from comedy to tragedy and back is something very few writers can or will ever accomplish. His drama's affect one both emotionally and psychologically and the verbal pyrotechnics seen in his sonnets are impossible to find anywhere else. All this makes him stand out as the lone, most famous writer of what is also known as "The Age of Shakespeare."

By the end of the 17th century, any variance from the use of Standard English or the use of another dialect began to be considered "uncivilized" and seen as signs of a lower class. Shakespeare himself began using these dialects as comic material in his work. By the end of the 18th century, it was clear that anybody who even spoke with a Cockney accent was going to be branded as a "vagabond!"

## 17 FAST FACT...

📖 **WILLIAM SHAKESPEARE** is estimated to have coined 2,000 neologisms (new words), and some are still in use, such as assassination, critical, hint, etc.

## 18 FAST FACT...

📖 **SHAKESPEARE** has not only composed and written a total of 154 sonnets and 37 plays in his lifetime, but also has performed as an actor in innumerous plays, mostly his own, but also in some others, such as those of Ben Johnson.

# FROM "MAY" AND "HOOSE" TO "ME" AND "HOUSE!"

**THE GREAT VOWEL SHIFT** was a radical change from the 15th to 18th centuries, and it affected the long vowel sounds. The sound of the long vowels began to be made from a place further forward and higher in the mouth. It was quite a sudden change in the English language.

It is believed that the shift took place in eight stages. During this period, the purer vowel sounds coming from European languages were done away with and the phonetic pairing between the long and short vowels was also lost.

The Shift is characterized by changes in a certain vowel that, in order to "keep its distance," pushes another vowel. There is the "push theory," which moved the lower vowel sounds forward and up. This led to the pushing of the others ahead. Similar was the "pull theory" in which the lower vowel sounds are "pulled" along by the upper vowel sounds that move first.

Not only did The Great Vowel Shift lead to the loss of connection between the English words and the foreign words they were derived from, but it also led to a lot of oddities in the pronunciation of English words. Sometimes, the spellings of words were changed to suit their new pronunciations, such as in the case of the word "life" which was earlier written as "lyf."

## 20 FAST FACT...

**IN THE 18TH CENTURY,** it was fashionable to pronounce a broad "a" in words like "bath," "dance," and "castle" to make them sound like "bahth", "dahnce", and "cahstle". This had nothing to do with the Great Vowel Shift.

## 21 FAST FACT...

**THE DIFFERENT PRONUNCIATIONS OF** "o" in the words "hove," "shove," and "move" is credited to the irregularities and regional variations that took place during the vowel shift, leading to a lack of uniformity in their pronunciation.

## JOHANNES GUTENBERG SETS UP THE FIRST PRINTING PRESS

**THE PRINTING PRESS WAS FIRST INVENTED** by Johannes Gutenberg around 1439 in Germany. Each letter's mirror image was carved in relief on a small block. Words were formed when the blocks, which were easily movable, were arranged to form different words. The words were separated with the help of blank spaces, and this gave rise to a line of type and a number of such lines of type gave rise to a page.

With the help of some borrowed money, Gutenberg started the "Bible Revolution" in the year 1452, wherein 200 copies of the two-volume Gutenberg Bible were printed, out of which only a small number of them were printed on vellum.

Johannes Gutenberg

## FAST FACT...

**BY YEAR 1500,** 13 million books were being circulated in Europe that was populated with 100 million people then.

## FAST FACT...

**THE GUTENBERG BIBLES** were expensive and beautiful, and were sold at the 1455 Frankfurt Book Fair, where each one was equal to the amount an average clerk got as his salary in three years. About 50 of these Bibles survive today.

# THE MAGIC OF MASS PRODUCTION

**THE ARRIVAL OF THE PRINTING PRESS IN ENGLAND** led to the development and spread of modern English, which began in full swing. The first printing press in England was established by William Caxton at Westminster Abbey in the year 1476. Caxton's translation of "The Recuyell of the Historyes of Troye" was the first book to be printed in the English language. The original was printed in Burges in 1473 or early 1474.

As the output of books increased due to mass production, the cost of books began to fall, and books became more commonly available in England. This made them available to a larger section of the population and thus led to a subsequent rise in literacy. Printing also helped to disseminate information and knowledge, and preserve knowledge.

## 26 POPULATION OF "VOWELS" WAS ON A RISE

**NOW THAT'S A TAD DIFFICULT TO BELIEVE,** isn't it? But it's true that facts are "really" stranger than fiction. And here's what actually happened in those dog-eared pages of English history.

Standardization nudged the use of more double vowels and standard punctuations. This was something that had not taken place until then. There was an increased use of double vowels (as in the word "soon").
The consonants, especially those towards the end of words began to decrease drastically.
Of course, this trend did not continue for long. But this was a massive change that is credited to initial standardization by printers.

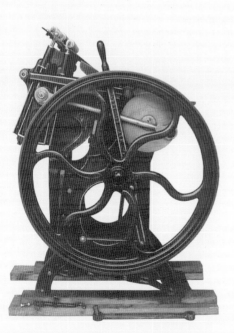

## 27 FAST FACT...

**ABOUT 20,000 BOOKS** ranging from poems, devotional pieces, grammar books, dictionaries, and mythical stories were printed in the 150 years that followed the year 1476, which was when the printing press arrived in England.

## 28 PRINTERS PAVE WAY FOR STANDARDIZATION

**THE CHANCERY** of Westminster around 1403 itself made some attempts to standardize English spellings and grammar by setting specific spellings and terms for official documents, such as using "land" instead of "lond" or using "I" in place of the personal pronoun "Ich." While that did help, it was the printing press that was truly responsible for the standardization of the language.

Once mass printing began, the spellings and dialect of London, the national capital, became the standard. That's because most publishing houses were located there. One of the major decisions made by the publishers, which had serious repercussions, was the use of the Northern English words "they," "their," and "them" instead of the words "hi," "his," and "hem," which were used in London.

But words were being printed before an orthographic agreement had risen among writers and teachers. This led to a large amount of variance in the spellings. Even so, by 1650, standardization had somewhat arrived.

# REFORMING THE PUNCTUATIONS

**A GREAT AMOUNT OF STANDARDIZATION** was seen with regards to punctuations in grammar by the 16th century. The virgule used in Middle English, which was an oblique stroke (/), a very common sign for punctuation, was replaced by the comma. Full stops were added only at the end of sentences and quotation marks were used to denote direct speech. Furthermore, capital letters were used for proper nouns, names, and at the beginning of a sentence. Semi colons were used too, though the exact rules of usage were not clear back then.

John Hart is to be given credit for a large number of these punctuation reforms. Unlike most other sections of English grammar that keeps undergoing changes on a continuous basis, punctuations introduced by John Hart have continued to remain the same since their introduction during the standardization phase.

William Shakespeare

## FAST FACT...

📖 **OVER 80 DIFFERENT SPELLINGS** of Shakespeare's name have been documented, and it is interesting to note that he has used different spellings in all his six known signatures.

# THOU SHALT KNOW THY PRONOUN!

**AROUND THE YEAR 1650,** the second person singular pronouns, namely all the "th" forms like, "thou," "thy," and "thee," got lost from upper class speech.

As seen in Shakespeare's "Hamlet," "you" was used to address someone respectfully and as the plural form. For example, while addressing a superior, an adult, when speaking to a stranger to whom one wanted to show respect they would use "you."

But with friends, inferiors, and children, the pronoun used was "thou." Thus, the use of "thou" and "thee" became close to unknown by the early 1700s. But it was still largely used while addressing God, as seen in the King James Bible and in a number of hymns.

With pronouns like "my" and "mine," "a" and "an," there was confusion about where the "n" belonged. Take the case of "mine uncle" and "my nuncle" and "an apron" or "a napron." The confusion cleared only by the 18th century when the distinction between "my" and "mine" was established. "My" became the possessive form and "mine" the nominal form.

## FAST FACT...

**THE WORD "PRONOUN" ORIGINATED** from the Latin word "pronomen" where "pro" meant "in place of" and "nomen" stood for "name or noun."

## 33 "I" AM SMALL NO MORE AND "HE" IS EVERYONE!

**IN AN EARLIER PERIOD,** "i" which was used to refer to one's self was written in the lower case. But in the course of time, the intellectual writers and readers realized that, in order to ensure that the use of "I" to refer to one's self was not confused with its use as a simple letter, there needed to be some form of distinction. Hence, around the early 1700s, "I" became capitalized so that it would stand out in texts.

Another interesting feature of English grammar that is practised even today is the use of male pronouns to refer to people as a whole, irrespective of their gender. Not many people are aware of the fact that the practice of using male pronouns such as "he", "his," and "him" for both males and females began in the 18th century.

Anne Fisher was the first grammarian to suggest the generic use of the male pronoun "he" for either sex.

## 34 FAST FACT...

**ANN FISHER** was the first woman to write a book on English grammar in 1745. Her book "A New Grammar With Exercises of Bad English" had 32 editions, making it one of the most popular guides of its time.

# 35 THE ENGLISH REFORMATION

**KING HENRY VII** wanted to annul his marriage to Catherine of Aragon due to her inability to conceive a male heir. But the Papal authority delayed the annulment due to her illicit extra-marital affair. This delay made the King impatient and he rejected the Papal authority.

After that, he set up the Anglican Church, which was to be The State Church of England. This split made the King the "Protector and Only Supreme Head of the Church and Clergy of England." And it all led to the infiltration of Protestant ideas into England. A number of Protestant Churches sprang up after this.

But it also changed the official attitude towards an "English" Bible. By the year 1539, several new Bibles were published in the English language. Two very important milestones in English literature came in the form of the "Book of Common Prayer" in 1549 and the "King James Bible."

Henry VII

The former was an English translation of the Church liturgy and the latter was a result of 200 years of effort to produce a Bible in England's native language and to standardize the enormous amount of new Bibles that had been published in the past 70 years.

## FAST FACT...

📖 **A COMMITTEE OF 54 CLERICS** and scholars compiled the King James Bible, which was published in 1611, and is still considered to be the conclusive English version of "The Bible" by many.

## FAST FACT...

📖 **CATHERINE OF ARAGON** was married to Arthur Tudor, King Henry's elder brother. On his death, he married Catherine who was 23 while he was 18.

## FAST FACT...

📖 **CATHERINE OF ARAGON** got pregnant six times with King Henry VII's child but only one survived beyond infancy (Mary I).

# RISE OF A TECHNOLOGICAL SOCIETY

**SOMEWHERE BETWEEN 1720 AND THE MIDDLE OF 1800**s, there was a switch from hand production methods to machine made products. This led to the creation of machine tools and equipment as well as the development of new kinds of materials and techniques. And in order to run heavy machinery, the Britishers came up with the idea of harnessing steam to generate power. New means of transportation as well as communication were discovered during this period called "The Industrial Revolution."

James Watt

It is said that at least half of the industrial and scientific advances were recorded in English. Along with England, the United States of America also helped establish English dominance by lending a hand in the field of new inventions and discoveries.

And so, late Modern English grammar saw the addition of many new words as new creations and discoveries. This gave rise to the need for neologisms. The scientists and scholars of the time largely depended on classical languages for the origin of new words. Words such as "chloroform," "nuclear," "oxygen," and "electron" all emerge from Latin and Greek roots. The plethora of "-ology" and "-onomy" words such as taxonomy and biology were also discovered and added to the English vocabulary during this period.

## 40 FAST FACT...

**JAMES WATT** invented the steam engine in 1781. That was fundamental to the changes that took place during the Industrial Revolution.

## 41 SELF-EXPLAINING COMPOUNDS AND THE "FIXES"

🎓 **APART FROM THE WORDS THAT WERE BORROWED** from Latin and Greek elements, there was a second source responsible for creating new words – amalgamations of already existing words in English. This led to the creation of "self-explaining compounds," one of the oldest methods of word formation.

## 42 FAST FACT

📖 **THE WORD "COUNTERATTACK"** came from World War I, and the word "counterintelligence" came from the World War II.

Another popular method for expanding the English vocabulary was appending prefixes and suffixes to existing words. Latin prefixes were easily used to create new combinations as in the case of the prefix "-trans," which led to the creation of words such as transliterate, transmarine, and transformer. Furthermore, suffixes such as "-less" and "-ful" were also added to existing words to create new ones.

## 43 RISE OF THE ACRONYMS

**THE NEXT STAGE** was the formation of acronyms. A few acronyms began being created during the 19th century. These were made by combining the initial letters of two or more words. Take the case of the word "Radar" (Radio Detecting And Ranging). Furthermore, certain words that were coined at that time were often analogies with other words in the English language, like "Mazola" comes from the words Maize and Oil.

Thus, we see that grammarians and scholars adopted various means and tactics other than pure invention of words to enhance the English vocabulary.

## 44 FAST FACT...

**THE WORD "KODAK"** is believed to have been coined by George Eastman in the year 1888 with the help of an anagrams set, and is a popular brand name even today.

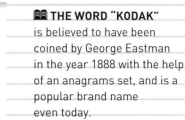

ORGANIZATION
DISTRIBUTION
POSITIONING
TEAMWORK
INVESTMENT
TECHNOLOGY

# I AM "PROPER" NO MORE!

**IN THE EARLY** 18th century, a large number of English words were being derived from names of people and places. Many have stuck on till today! The word "sandwich" owes its existence to the Earl of Sandwich, who, on a particular occasion, put a slice of meat in between two pieces of bread.

### FAST FACT...

**THE WORD "SIDEBURNS"** is named after General Ambrose Burnside.

### FAST FACT...

**THE WORD "CARDIGAN"** comes from The Earl of Cardigan.

In the same way, words for newly invented things took up the inventor's name. For example, the word "colt" which is a kind of firearm takes up after its inventor Samuel Colt. We get the word "tabasco sauce" from the River Tabasco in Mexico.

Here's an interesting story about how the word "boycott" got coined. In 1880, Captain Boycott, an Irish owner's agent refused to accept rents at what the tenants had set it. He was threatened with murder, his servants were made to leave forcefully, and they even burnt his figure in effigy.

That's what gave rise to the verb "boycott," meaning "coercing a person by refusing to and preventing others from dealing with him."

## 48 ENGLISH — THE LANGUAGE OF THE WORLD!

**BETWEEN THE 18TH AND 20TH CENTURY,** British Colonialism gained large amounts of momentum even though it began as early as the 16th century. The British established their colonies in places like India (with establishment of East India Company for trade), The Caribbean (because of sugar and tobacco plantations and slaves), New Zealand (for trade in food, weapons, and metal tools) and South Africa (which served as a port and for gold and diamonds discovered later). They even ruled places like Canada, Australia, Singapore, and Egypt. At the height of British colonialism, almost one-fourth of the earth's surface was under British rule.

The extension of the English language to the backward and underdeveloped countries of Africa and Asia was seen as a desirable thing by British rulers. They saw it as a chance to impose it on all colonies. This was done to bind the colonies closely and create some order in the chaotic regions.

The colonies were quite happy to be able to learn English as this enabled them to profit from the technological and scientific advances of the British. It was the settlers, traders, administrators, merchants, soldiers, and missionaries who settled or visited the various colonies that facilitated the spread of the English language.

## 49 FAST FACT...

**GERMAN LINGUIST, JACOB GRIMM** predicted that English was "the language of the world" and was "destined to reign in future with still more extensive sway over all parts of the globe."

## 50 FAST FACT...

**THE NUMBER OF "MOTHER-TONGUE ENGLISH SPEAKERS"** at the close of the 16th century was 5-7 million, all in Britain. This number increased about 50-fold in the next 350 years, and about 80% of them lived outside Britain.

## 51 LOANWORDS AND "NEW ENGLISHES!"

**BRITISH DEALINGS** with exotic countries due to a general increase in trade led to the inclusion of a large number of borrowed or "loanwords" into the English language. British officers caught onto slang words heard from cotton traders in India, vendors selling street food in the Caribbean, or from warriors fighting the Britons. This may be the reason why we use certain words even today, for they would carry these new words back to London and thus spread them.

Certain words that the English language and its grammar picked up from colonies all over were very useful locally, but in general were quite pointless. Examples of such words are boomerang, kangaroo, and budgerigar that entered the English language from Australia, but are restricted to the region. On the other hand, certain colonies gave the language very common everyday words, such as India, from where words like pajamas, bungalow, jungle, shampoo, candy, and many others were borrowed.

The rise of the modern dialects (such as Australian English, South African English, etc.) which were referred to as "New Englishes" is what led people like Noah Webster to predict the future fragmentation of the English language into mutually indiscernible languages. This had been seen with Latin, which gave rise to Italian, French, and Spanish. However, it is safe to say that this has not happened and will not happen to the English language in the future.

NAM

Bloemfontein
De Aar

LES.

Richards B

Durbar

**SOUTH AFRICA**

'LANTIC
'CEAN

Saldanha

East London

Cape Town

Port Elizabeth

Mossel Bay

INDIAN
OCEAN

## 52 FAST FACT...

📖 **NOAH WEBSTER** had predicted "a language in North America as different from the future language of England as modern Dutch, Danish, and Swedish are from German or from one another".

## 53 FAST FACT...

📖 **THE WORD "ZIPPER"** was first patented by B. F. Goodrich Company, but soon became the common word and term used to refer to the mechanism in general.

## 54 FAST FACT...

📖 **NOBEL-WINNING AUTHOR J.M. COETZEEÕS NOVEL "FOE"** in 1986 is believed to be woven around Robinson Crusoe's plot.

# ROBINSON CRUSOE

📖 **THE LIFE AND STRANGE SURPRISING ADVENTURES OF ROBINSON CRUSOE,** of York, Mariner: Who lived Eight and Twenty Years, all alone in an un-inhabited Island on the Coast of America, near the Mouth of the Great River of Oroonoque; Having been cast on Shore by Shipwreck, wherein all the Men perished but himself. With An Account how he was at last as strangely deliver'd by Pirates." Phew! Yes, that was the original title of Daniel Defoe's Robinson Crusoe.

It was inspired by a Scottish sailor Alexander Selkirk, who lived on a Pacific Island called Más a Tierra for four years. Defoe dramatized the experience of living on a deserted island for 28 years in his novel which was the fictional autobiography of the protagonist Robinson Crusoe as he survives on the tropical island and encounters various things like cannibals, mutineers, and prisoners before being rescued. What is interesting to know is that the island that Alexander was on is now called "Robinson Crusoe Island."

Defoe is known to have written a sequel to the book called "The Farther Adventures of Robinson Crusoe," but it is not nearly as popular as the first one. Classic Illustrated also published the story in a comic book form in 1943 and 1957.

Daniel Defoe

## FAST FACT...

📖 **DANIEL DEFOE,** who was considered the father of British Journalism, was also imprisoned seven times during his life due to his political passion and because he was almost always in debt.

## THE BIRTH OF THE "MAN-FRIDAY"

**57**

👨‍🎓 **ROBINSON CRUSOE WAS WRITTEN IN A DIDACTIC** and confessional form, and had a journalistic detail and characterization. With his simple narrative style of writing, Daniel Defoe managed to make a lasting impression on the literary world. It was published in 1719 but even before the end of the year, four editions of the first volume had been run through.

This book is believed to have begun the realistic fiction genre in literature, and the grammar was influenced accordingly. "Robinsonade" was the term coined to describe this genre of stories. By the end of the 19th century, no book in history had more spin offs, translations, and editions than Robinson Crusoe. In addition to all this, the book found various adaptations, of itself for stage, film, as well as for television.

### FAST FACT...

**58**

📖 **ROBINSON CRUSOE** has over 700 alternative versions, such as children's versions, and has been translated into languages like Coptic and Maltese as well.

### FAST FACT...

**59**

📖 **IN 1796,** a pantomime version of Robinson Crusoe was staged at Theatre Royal and in 1927 a silent film called "Robinson Crusoe" was also made.

One of the greatest legacies of this book is the word "Man-Friday." Friday was one of the character's in Defoe's novel who got his name because that was the day on which he met Robinson Crusoe. They were unable to communicate with one another at first and so Crusoe named him Friday. This character was the source of the popular term "Man-Friday" which is a term used to refer to a loyal and competent servant or assistant.

# THE ROMANTIC ERA

**ROMANTICISM WAS A LITERARY MOVEMENT THAT ORIGINATED** in Europe at the end of the 18th century and swept through almost every country peaking between 1800 and 1850. The essential spirit of romanticism was aimed against the order of things that had been established, such as the precise rules and dogmas as well as the laws. The romantics reacted against the socio-political norms set up during the "Age of Enlightenment," and also revolted against the impersonality of industrialization.

William Blake

Romanticism influenced England mostly between the end of the 18th century until 1870. Here, it was primarily expressed through poetry. The Romantic Movement was slightly delayed in reaching America, and peaked between 1830 and the end of the Civil War. In contrast to England, it was the novel that served as the most befitting mode of expression for romanticism.

It is important to understand that the romantic movement believed in the supremacy of imagination over reason, emotions over logic, as well as intuitive thinking over the scientific way of life. This paved the way for the creation of a large body of literature focusing on passion and sensibility. Prior to this era, there were very stern expectations with regards to the content as well as a poem's structure, especially during the Neoclassical Period of the 18th century. Romanticism allowed for the loosening up of these rules and allowed artists to experiment with new styles and subjects. The previous generation poets used high-flown vocabulary, which was replaced by easy and more natural verbosity and cadences.

In fact, an important change that was seen during this period was that the rhythmic stanza used in poetry then was giving way to blank verse which was style, wherein conversational speech was hoisted up to levels of absolute beauty.

## 61 FAST FACT...

📖 **WILLIAM WORDSWORTH** was orphaned at an early age and suffered from anosmia, an inability to smell.

## 62 FAST FACT...

📖 **ONE OF WILLIAM WORDSWORTH'S** greatest works "The Prelude" was not published during his lifetime.

## 63 FAST FACT...

📖 **WILLIAM WORDSWORTH** would lie down on the ground outside with his daughter and act like they were lying in their grave.

William Wordsworth

# THE BRITISH ROMANTICS

🎓 **ONE OF THE** most creative men of his generation, and a seminal figure during the Romantic Era, William Blake was one of the first writers to concentrate on content instead of form. Although he struggled for the majority of his life and remained relatively unknown, he was way ahead of his times. He was deeply affected by the Industrial Revolution and the plight of the common workers and this aided his creative process and led to one of his greatest work – "Songs of Innocence and Experience" compiled in the 1790s. It is said that the Old and New Testament were his inspiration but it was Blake's taste that transformed the stories of the Bible into something completely fresh and original. He was greatly misunderstood by his contemporaries and was sometimes even considered mad due to his unstable temper.

## FAST FACT...

📖 **WILLIAM BLAKE** told people that when he was four he saw God who put up his head on the window. And at age 12 he said he saw a tree full of angels.

If one was to name a single poet who truly upheld the standards of Romanticism, it would undoubtedly be William Wordsworth. His publication in 1798 of Lyrical Ballads is considered by many as the starting point of the Romantic Movement. The dominant theme that ran through it was nature and its ability to influence human imagination and mind. The primary source of his poetry and inspiration he said was "The infinite variety of natural appearances." Wordsworth defined poetry as "the spontaneous overflow of powerful feelings" and "emotion recollected in tranquility."

Percy Bysshe Shelley, with his "Ode to the West Wind," and John Keats, known for his "Ode on a Grecian Urn," too are well-known romantics of the period.

# ROMANTICISM ELUCIDATED

🎓 **ONE OF THE MOST IMPORTANT THINGS TO UNDERSTAND ABOUT ROMANTICISM** is that it is concerned with the individual more than with society. What fascinated Romantics the most was individual consciousness and imagination. The idea of "romantic originality" illustrates this, as the key to Romanticism is the idea that the artist must produce his original work through the process of "creation from nothingness."

It embodied the belief that emotions were equally, if not more important than, reason as opposed to the Enlightenment method of thinking, and allowed for the liberation of feelings.

The Romantics also showed a strong belief and interest in the importance of nature. A large number of them believed in nature being the abode of God, and that God and natural universe were one and the same. Thus, they perceived nature as sublime, and as a means for self discovery. They believed that a close connection with nature was healthy, morally and mentally, and thus many of them wrote about nature or when they were surrounded by it.

Isaiah Berlin very beautifully explained romanticism in a nutshell by saying that Romanticism embodied "a new and restless spirit, seeking violently to burst through old and cramping forms, a nervous preoccupation with perpetually changing inner states of consciousness, a longing for the unbounded and the indefinable, for perpetual movement and change, an effort to return to the forgotten sources of life, a passionate effort at self-assertion both individual and collective, and a search after means of expressing an unappeasable yearning for unattainable goals."

## FAST FACT...

📖 **JOHN KEATS** died of tuberculosis, which he had caught from his brother Tom while he was nursing him to health.

John Keats

## 68 HARBINGERS OF AMERICAN ROMANTICISM

🎓 **THE MIDDLE OF 19TH CENTURY IS KNOWN AS THE AMERICAN RENAISSANCE** in literature, although nobody took note of the growing creativity and flourishing literature back then. Even romantic novelists such as Nathaniel Hawthorne and Herman Melville, who are regarded as classics today, remained practically unknown throughout their lives. But they were coming up with greatly symbolic and original works. They took their cues from the English Renaissance, but there was darkness to the American Romanticism. And that made it distinctly separate from it.

Arguably the greatest poet in American literary history, Walt Whitman and his "Leave of Grass" (1855), marked a turning point in the history of poetry. His sources of inspiration were similar to those of others, but he showed a spirit of democracy and inclusion of people from around the world.

Credited for being the inventor of detective fiction and the original master of horrors, Edgar Allen Poe explored the strange and weirder side of human nature. Poe's dreary settings, exploration of the grotesque, and his sing song way of writing earned him quite a lot of criticism, and yet he is considered to be the most purely Romantic poet and story writer of his time.

## 69 FAST FACT...

📖 **AFTER NATHANIEL'S DEATH,** H.W. Longfellow wrote a poem titled "Hawthorne" to pay homage to his friend's creativity.

American Romanticism resulted in the further development of the grammar of American English, which was steadily developing visible differences compared to its source of origination.

## 70 FAST FACT...

📖 **HAWTHORNE WROTE "THE SCARLET LETTER"** lamenting the death of his mother. At first when he took it to the publisher, he was told that it was too short.

## 71 FAST FACT...

📖 **WALT WHITMAN** ate four raw eggs for breakfast everyday for the last 20 years of his life.

Edgar Allen Poe

## 72 FAST FACT...

📖 **WALT WHITMANŌS "LEAVES OF GRASS"** was originally published with his own money, and was criticized greatly due to its overt sexuality.

## 73 FAST FACT...

📖 **EDGAR ALLEN POE** earned only $9 for his famous "The Raven."

# AUGUSTAN LITERATURE – A STORY OF WIT AND SATIRE

**THE STYLE OF LITERATURE THAT DEVELOPED** in the early half of the 18th century is often referred to as "Augustan Literature."

The term "Augustan" comes from King George I's wish to be compared to the first Roman Emperor, Augustus Ceasar. Under his reign, poetry and other arts were admired and supported. They bloomed due to his support.

Augustan literature was structured according to norms that governed Greek and Roman works and was classical in style. The primary philosophy of this era was empiricism, which is the reliance on reasoning and proof.

Some of the distinguishing features of this type of literature were domination of wit, excessive popularity of satire, evolution of the novel, use of classical and biblical allusions in writing (like Paradise Lost), and the change from political satire to clear melodrama.

But there's one more characteristic – and this one's really interesting – that defines the period of Augustan literature. It's the fact that most authors used to criticize other fellow authors. So much so that plays were written to spite or make fun of other successful plays. Talk about being competitive!

Jonathan Swift

## FAST FACT...

**THIS ERA IN LITERATURE** is believed to have ended with the deaths of its two most influential writers - Alexander Pope and Jonathan Swift in 1744 and 1745 respectively.

## FAST FACT...

**JOHN LOCKE** was the man who championed the philosophy of empiricism during the Restoration Period.

# STALWARTS OF AUGUSTAN LITERATURE

🎓 **ALEXANDER POPE IS KNOWN TO HAVE DOMINATED THE POETIC GENRE** of the Augustan period and some of his proverbs and couplets are used as axioms up until now in modern English. Pope was highly quarrelsome in print and although he did not have many poetic enemies, he had quite a few personal, religious, and philosophical opponents. Pope wrote "The Dunciad" in 1728, ridiculing his contemporary enemies and they came to be referred to as "The Dunces" due to his successful satirizing of them in it. He often quarreled and argued over what should be considered as proper subjects in poetry. One of Pope's other satirical masterpieces is The Rape of Locke," which he wrote in 1712 and 1714. It is a mock-heroic narrative poem that ridicules classical literature with their Gods, nymphs, and heroes.

King George I

## 78 FAST FACT...

📖 **AN EMPIRICAL APPROACH** can be clearly seen in the effort of Samuel Johnson to pin down the exact meaning of words in his "Dictionary of the English Language" (1755).

## 79 FAST FACT...

📖 **KING GEORGE I** ascended the throne of England at the age of 54 and did not know English when he first ascended the throne, for he was originally from Germany.

In 18th century prose satire, there is but one man who overshadows all others and that is poet and novelist, Jonathan Swift. Swift's satire ranged over all kinds of topics and what he did was combine satire with parody. His first major satire was "The Tale of Tub" written from 1703-1705, which spoke of the old and new conception of values. His most significant satire "Gulliver's Travels" is an excellent example of Augustan Literature, and is believed to be an appraisal of human vanity. Other important names during this era were Samuel Richardson, who wrote "Pamela" and "Clarissa" as well as Henry Fielding, who parodied Samuel in his work "Shamela" and wrote "Joseph Andrews" and "Tom Jones."

An illustration from
Gulliver's Travels

## FAST FACT...

📖 **THE COMMONLY** used adages—"To err is human, to forgive divine," and "A little learning is a dangerous thing" are both phrases from Pope's "Essay on Criticism."

## FAST FACT...

📖 **ALEXANDER POPE** suffered from a tubercular disease in his childhood and never grew taller than 4 feet 6 inches. He suffered from curvature of the spine and headaches.

## FAST FACT...

📖 **GULLIVER'S TRAVELS** was originally named – "Travels into Several Remote Nations of the World, in Four Parts. By Lemuel Gulliver, First a Surgeon, and then a Captain of Several Ships."

Alexander Pope

# THE VICTORIAN ERA AND THE RISE OF NOVELS!

**🎓 THE PERIOD BETWEEN 1837 AND 1901** is referred to as the Victorian Era in Great Britain. Queen Victoria was the ruling monarchy during these years. Changing styles in grammar were deeply influenced by the changing social conditions in Great Britain. Sentences grew shorter and precise, the language adapted to include a tone that the common man could relate to. Great novelists such as Charles Dickens and George Eliot belonged to this era. Their novels often had a common theme that centered around the hardships of the commoners. In the latter part of the Victorian era, the novels began to get a lot more complicated in nature with a lot more characters.

Charles Dickens

The grammar during this era included long sentences with lots of phrases and idioms. The early novels of the period – just like "Pickwick Papers," which was Charles Dickens' first novel – were quite poetic in their writing style.

The Victorian Era also observed the rise of writers from British colonies such as Australia, United States of America, and New Zealand. They gradually developed their own style and grammar for their novels, which influenced the English spoken in their countries.

## 84 FAST FACT...

📖 **APART FROM** Charles Dickens' novels, Emily Bronte's "Wuthering Heights" and William Makepeace Thackeray's "Vanity Fair" are among the greatest classics of the Victorian era.

## THE "INVENTION OF CHILDHOOD!"

**YES, WE KNOW** that it's practically impossible to "invent" childhood. Yet, the phrase tagged along with the Victorian era. And here's why.

In this era, the novels and poetries were specifically directed towards children. The socio-political conditions were responsible for the practice. And that's because child labor was rampant in Britain. Major efforts were being made to educate children.

The writers of this period contributed to the movement by giving rise to children's literature. The grammar of the Victorian era was also deeply influenced by the addition of words and metaphors that were light-hearted, and could be easily digested by a child.

As literacy levels rose among children, literature for young people became an interesting prospect for writers. Famous adult writers of the times were Charles Dickens and Robert Louis Stevenson. There were also writers like Lewis Caroll and Anna Sewell, who specifically wrote novels and poetry for young readers.

### FAST FACT...

**THE "RABBIT'S HOLE"** from Alice in Wonderland by Lewis Caroll was an actual name coined by children for the stairs at the back of the main hall at Christ Church.

## THE ORIGIN OF SPIDERMAN AND SUPERMAN!

🎓 **EVER WONDER WHO THOUGHT** of a boy who could spin a web like a spider, or a guy who fly like a bird? The answer lies in the Victorian era. The section of literature called "fantastic fiction" first came into existence in the 19th century. Noted English grammarians and literary figureheads of even modern times often credit the "fantastic fiction" of the Victorian Era for inspirations, which have led to the birth of modern day superheroes such as Spiderman and Superman!

Old Gothic tales such as the famous "The Old English Baron" by Clara Reeve were first penned down in the late 18th century. Gothic tales were characterized by witchcraft, ghosts, and curses, and were often based in castles, cemeteries, or monasteries.

A lot of the other tales that were passed down from generation to generation up to that point in time were penned down by other writers. Apart from these tales that were centuries old, supernatural characters came into existence. Some of these characters are still very popular among people of all generations. These superheroes generally had dominating enemies who were very sophisticated and quite difficult to beat. The underlying moral was always that of the victory of "good over evil."

## 88 FAST FACT...

📖 **YOU WOULD BE SURPRISED** to note that the legendary "Sherlock Holmes," created by the legendary Sir Arthur Conan Doyle is a great example of the "supernatural" fiction of the Victorian Era that has come to define future superheroes.

## 89 FAST FACT...

📖 **H.G. WELLS WROTE** "The Invisible Man." Other fictional characters with supernatural abilities like "Phileas Fogg," "Sexton Blake," and "Dracula" among several others were products of the Victorian Era.

# "ALICE IN WONDERLAND" AND "NONSENSE VERSE"

**ANOTHER IMPORTANT ADDITION** that took place in the Victorian era was the birth of the "nonsense verse." This is actually a form of rhythmic, light-hearted humor that often forms a part of poetry or novels for children. It is used to describe strange characters in very funny and supernatural situations. Limericks are a very common example of "nonsense verse."

Lewis Caroll, Mervyn Peake, and Colin West are English writers who are extremely popular for their "nonsense verses." It is interesting to note that "Alice's Adventures in Wonderland" by Lewis Caroll is probably the most popular novel known for its nonsense verse even today. When it was first released in 1865, it became a rage among both adults and children.

The story of Alice falling down a rabbit hole into a peculiar, unrealistic but interesting world called "Wonderland" where she met some unbelievably weird creatures like "The Mad Hatter," "The Cheshire Cat," and "The Queen of Hearts" continues to be popular for its narrative, characters, imagery, and most importantly, its play with logic! Interestingly, its sequel called "Through the Looking Glass" was not as popular.

## FAST FACT...

**LEWIS CAROLL** kept records of everything he did, even the letters he wrote. He wrote 98,721 letters between January 1861 and his death in 1898!

## FAST FACT...

**MOCK TURTLE** soup which is talked about in Alice in Wonderland was a soup in the Victorian era made from parts of calf.

# THE SUFFRAGE MOVEMENT AND WOMEN EMPOWERMENT

🎓 **ENGLISH GRAMMAR AND LITERATURE** in the 19th century and the early 20th century was deeply impacted by the Suffrage Movement. The word "suffragette" was first used in an article in a British newspaper in 1906. It was used to describe women who were heavily campaigning for the right to vote, which was denied to them. This practice had begun in the early 19th century itself. In 1903, Emmeline Pankhurst and her daughters Christabel and Sylvia founded the Women's Social and Political Union (WSPU).

Suffrage women

The Suffrage Movement became more militant once WSPU was created. It started with women and protesters chaining themselves to railings around the Prime Minister's residence. But in the course of time, protesters began smashing windows until the movement resulted in full blown riots and demonstrations.

Several great female writers of the time, such as the great Jane Austen supported this movement with their works, which showed the transforming situation of women who were becoming more independent, empowered, and ready to fight for the rights.

## FAST FACT...

📖 **WOMEN PROTESTER** groups during the Suffrage movement were the first to picket the White House. Since then, this protest step has been replicated by many.

# "EMMA" AND OTHER WOMAN ORIENTED WORKS

🎓 **AS THE SUFFRAGE MOVEMENT SPREAD** across different countries of the world, woman oriented works by great female authors and supporters of the "suffrage movement" became very popular. Some of these books written in earlier times, such as "Emma" by Jane Austen in 1815 became a source of inspiration for the protesters.

On seeing the condescending nature of her brother John Knightley towards her sister Isabella, who was married to him, Emma decides that she never wants to get married. She wants to be free from the control of her husband and live her life on her own terms. This is seen as one of the works that marked the beginning of woman empowerment in English literature and grammar.

Another one "The House of Mirth" written by Edith Wharton is another legendary book that shows the social standing of women in that period. The book describes how the unequal standing of women as compared to men affects them. The inability to support herself, her value being judged only by her beauty, and her inability to take her own decisions destroy Lily, the main protagonist at the end of the book.

## FAST FACT...

📖 **THE WORKS AND OTHER IDEAS** for women empowerment such as those spread through the monthly magazine, "Housekeeping Monthly" inspired women.

# THE RISE OF FEMINIST LITERATURE

**INITIALLY, THE SCOPE OF WRITING** that the women stuck to was related to domestic situations which were very women centric. However, as the 19th century progressed, women started becoming more and more bold in their style of writing and began to cover all the different spheres of life. Women wrote less about domestic conditions and more about the rights they deserved, their challenges in a male-dominated world, and the right to power. Thus, the real feminist literature came into existence.

Charlotte Brontë

Authors such as George Eliot, Charlotte Bronte among several others often received negative reviews from critics simply due to their woman centric nature of content or their gender.

A lot of women also began to write essays about women empowerment. Lillie Blake's articles in 1971, "Put Us In Your Place" and "Who Shall Be Ruler" became very popular. Other interesting and popular essays include "A Doll's House," "The Women of Tomorrow" and "A Bundle of Fallacies."

## 98 FAST FACT...

**THE SONG OF JOAN OF ARC,** written in 1429, is also considered to be feminist in nature.

## 99 FAST FACT...

**THE FIRST WAVE OF** feminism started in 1840 after Elizabeth Cady Stanton and Lucretia Mott were denied seats in the World Anti-Slavery Convention in London. This was the beginning of feminist literature, too.

# FROM ENGLISH TO GLOBISH!

**THOUGH THE SEEDS FOR ENGLISH TO FLOURISH** as a language all across the world were sown by the rampant colonization of the Britishers, English can be considered to have become the chief language globally only since the middle of the 20th century.

A large part of the world was under English colonization until World War II broke out, people in these areas already understood and spoke English. This helped English become a global language.

The most important factor was the rise of the era of technology and computers. The programming languages that computers understand are all in English. For programmers to learn these computer languages, they need to know basic English.

Other factors include the popularity of Hollywood films, the spread of Western Music, which is predominantly in English, and of course, the outsourcing of work by developed countries like the United States of America and Great Britain to Asian countries.

Efforts are now being made to set an international standard for the "many Englishes" spoken across the world. This new standard will be called Globish!

## FAST FACT...

**INDIA HAS SLOWLY** and steadily developed its own English dialect which is a combination of Hindi and English. It is called "Hinglish."

## FAST FACT...

**CHINA HAS MORE** English speaking people than the United States of America!

# THE GREAT CHARLES DICKENS OF PORTSMOUTH

**CHARLES DICKENS IS CONSIDERED** to be among the greatest English writers of all time. He wrote several novels, essays, poems, and letters, and even edited a weekly journal for over 20 years.

Dickens had a tough childhood that he never really spoke about, but some of his work subtly talks about the hardships he went through as a child. Even though he was poor, he went to school, but had to drop out early in order to support his family when his father was imprisoned. While he was working through his formative years, he suffered from loneliness and hardships.This aspect is often brought to play in his work. Through his works, he also campaigned vigorously for social reforms such as children's rights and education.

Charles Dickens

His writing style was defined by realism, fluency of prose, and genius for satiric caricature. Famous writers like Leo Tolstoy and George Orwell have greatly praised him for these facets of his writing. His style of using names for his characters which were heavily based on their characteristics inspired many. For example, the name "Mr. Murdstone" for a character in David Copperfield gives the feeling of "death" and "stony coldness."

## FAST FACT...

**"A DINNER AT POPLAR WALK"** published in "Monthly Magazine" in December, 1833 was Charles Dickens' first published story.

## FAST FACT...

**CHARLES DICKENS** was an active member of The Ghost Club. He was extremely interested in the paranormal, though he did not write many books about this subject.

## THE LEGENDARY "THOMAS JEFFERSON SNODGRASS" A.K.A MARK TWAIN!

**MARK TWAIN WAS A CONTEMPORARY OF CHARLES DICKENS** and is widely revered to be among the greatest American authors of all time. His greatest works are "The Adventures of Tom Sawyer" and "The Adventures of Huckleberry Finn." His formative years in Hannibal, Missouri, provided the setting for these two great novels.

Mark Twain's original name was Samuel Langhorne Clemens. He used several pen names such as "Josh" and "Thomas Jefferson Snodgrass" before finally settling on Mark Twain around 1870. He wrote about several diverse topics which included the hypocritical nature of humans, their violent acts, and their vanities as well. His light-hearted and humorous verses are considered some of the best ever written.

Some of his other great novels include "The Prince and the Pauper," "Tom Sawyer Abroad," and "A Horse's Tale." Some of his greatest short stories are "Luck, A Dog's Tale," and "A Literary Nightmare." A lot of his works have gotten lost due to his habit of using several different pen names.

## FAST FACT...

📖 **AMERICAN AUTHOR** Ernest Hemmingway considered "The Adventures of Huckleberry Finn" as the greatest American novel of all times. He said, "If you read it, you must stop where Jim is stolen from the boys. That is the real end. The rest is just cheating." And he also said, "All modern American literature comes from one book by Mark Twain called Huckleberry Finn."

## FAST FACT...

📖 **HALEY'S COMET** is believed to have been visible on the birth date as well as death date of Mark Twain.

## FAST FACT...

📖 **MARK TWAIN HAS** also written five travelogues, which are about his travels from Western U.S.A to Asia.

# THE PHONOGRAPH — A REVOLUTIONARY INVENTION

**SEVERAL AGENTS OF COMMUNICATION** came up in the middle of 19th century. While the telegraph, the typewriter, and the press were sources of communication of the written word, the telephone, invented by Alexander Graham Bell, was a source of spoken communication. There was, however, no device up to then that could be used to reproduce sounds of different kinds. While carrying out his work on the inventions of the telegraph and the telephone, Edison also invented the phonograph.

The Edison Speaking Phonograph Company was then founded and these phonographs were soon available commercially. The uses for the phonograph included dictation without a stenographer, teaching of elocution, phonographic books for the blind, reproduction of music, educational application, and the preservation of languages through the recording of accurate pronunciations.

But it was not until others like Alexander Bell improved the original design that it became a revolutionary mode of recording and reproducing music, poetry, speeches, etc.

## 111 FAST FACT...

📖 **THE LITERAL MEANING** of the word "phonograph" is "writing sound," and it is a word of Greek origin. The phonograph was among Edison's favorite inventions.

Thomas Alwa Edison

## 112 FAST FACT...

📖 **INTERESTINGLY,** when he first tested the phonograph, he tested it by reciting the nursery rhyme "Mary Had a Little Lamb." To his amazement, the device played the words back to him in the exact way that he had recited them!

## 113 FROM "ACTIVE" TO "PASSIVE" VOICE

**THE 19TH CENTURY ALSO WITNESSED** various other developments in English grammar. Notable among them was that of passive voice. Passive voice began to be used more commonly in spoken English. This important grammatical structure suddenly began to appear in every form of written and spoken English.

Every English sentence is either in active voice or passive voice. In an active sentence, the person or thing is credited for the action. The sentence where person or thing which is acted upon is a passive sentence.

Passive voice, especially progressive passive voice (Past, Present, and Future), became a very common part of English language and grammar when it came to bureaucratic writing among many other places. Whenever an admission was to be made without giving further details about the person or thing responsible for it, passive voice began being used. For example – Mistakes were made! or Admission was refused.

## 114 FAST FACT...

**IN MODERN TIMES,** it is quintessential to master the art of converting active voice to passive voice and vice versa.

STALWARTS

GERMANIC

LATIN

NORMAN
FRENCH

# DICTIONARIES

## 501

# Key events in the evolution of Grammar - A Timeline

FRENCH

NORSE

# THE WEST GERMANIC ROOTS OF THE 5TH CENTURY

**WEST GERMANIC IS CONSIDERED TO BE THE FATHER OF ENGLISH** and was brought into Britain by the Angles, Saxons, and the Jutes, who came to help the Britons battle against the Picts and Scots in the early 5th century. Then, they settled down in Britain itself. English was different from other West Germanic languages like German and Dutch. These settlers referred to their language as "English" and their place of settlement as "England" by the early 8th century.

Their English, which is referred to as "Old English," was derived from ancient Germanic. There were nouns of different types, which belonged to three different genders-masculine, feminine, and neutral. All these nouns had four case endings, namely nominative, accusative, dative, and genitive.

One feature that distinguished Old English from most Asian languages of that time was the fact that verbs, nouns, pronouns, and adjectives always indicated whether they were singular or plural. This continues to be the case even today. Many of these features of English grammar continue to be a part of Modern English as well.

## FAST FACT

116

**SYNTAX OR WORD ORDER** did not play a major role in determining or giving meaning to sentences.

# NORSE INFLUENCES FROM THE 9TH CENTURY ONWARDS

**IN 835,** the Viking invasion of England played a major role in the evolution of English grammar. Initially, the Vikings simply invaded, looted, and plundered parts of England. However, by the late 8th century, the Vikings began settling down in England. And thus, the next phase in the development of English grammar began.

While English was a West Germanic language, the Vikings spoke Norse which was a North Germanic language. Since both languages originated from ancient Germanic, they were closely related. Hence, Norse began influencing the verbs, nouns, and pronouns in English. Among the most conspicuous changes that came about was the change in the verb "to be." The erstwhile "irregular and defective" verb form was replaced by the Norse verb form. Hence, the Norse influenced English and had people saying "They are" and not "they be" as was the case in the earlier times.

The third person present tense form also underwent changes courtesy Norse influences. So "he walketh" became "he walks" and "he cometh" became "he comes." It is also widely believed that sentences became structured, and the method of forming a question in English was developed courtesy Norse influences by introducing the reversal of the subject-verb order. So "I am' became "am I?" in question form.

Third person plural pronouns of the times were replaced by the Norse analogues. So "hi, hem, hir" became "they, them, their" respectively. Due to a lack of written records, there is not a lot known about further Norse influences on English grammar.

## FAST FACT...

📖 **THE WORD "BANDANNA"** is actually a word that is derived from the Hindi word "bandhna," which means to tie a scarf around the head.

## FAST FACT...

📖 **KNIFE AND KNOT** and a lot of other words, in which the "k" at the beginning is silent, are of Norse origin.

## FAST FACT...

📖 **MOST ANGLO SAXON** origin words in English start with the letter "b." For example, braid, brainy, bramble.

## FAST FACT...

📖 **BILL BRYSON** has often referred to the French invasion of England as "the final cataclysm (which) awaited the English language."

## 122 THE NORMAN FRENCH INFLUENCES POST THE 10ᵗʰ CENTURY

🎓 **THE ARRIVAL** of the Norman French in the middle of the 11ᵗʰ century, who settled and occupied England for a long time, resulted in major changes taking place in English grammar. Old English of the Viking period blended with the Norman French spoken by the invaders, resulting in an almost new form of English altogether!

During this period, almost all noun endings were lost. Logical gender replaced grammatical gender. Word order or syntax became significantly important in giving meaning to sentences. It was during this period that English underwent evolution from its pure Germanic roots of the times. Due to the influences of Norman French, English is the least Germanic dialect among all the different Germanic languages like Dutch, German, and Icelandic.

By 1400, English had replaced French as the most widely spoken language in England. In 1500, the English dialect that became the most common among all of them was Westminster English. Speaking this dialect was considered to be a matter of great prestige.

A lot of Norman French words found their way into the English language. In today's times, it is believed that over 30% of all English words are of French origin. Words like "joy," "joyous," "attaché," and several others found their way into English courtesy Norman French.

## 123 FAST FACT...

📖 **THE ENGLISH THAT WE ARE** acquainted with in modern times only came into existence around 300 years after the Norman French had occupied England and influenced the grammar of pre-Norman English.

# THE DOWNFALL OF LATIN BY THE 17ᵀᴴ CENTURY

🎓 **ONE OF THE CHIEF EVENTS** in the history of English grammar's evolution was the decline of Latin. Until the beginning of the 17ᵗʰ century, Latin was the language of the church, the writers, and science. But after that, first English dictionaries were seen and the concept of "English grammar" was introduced. "Grammar" to the people of England till then simply meant "Latin grammar."

Initially, English grammar was deeply influenced by Latin grammar, due to which there were a lot of shortcomings seen in it. Just like in Latin, no double negatives could be used, no sentences ended in prepositions, no comparatives could be used, and infinitives could not be split either. English was looked upon as a derivative of Latin, and inferior grammatically to not only Latin but also a lot of other foreign languages.

## FAST FACT

📖 **WRITERS LIKE** John Milton, William Shakespeare, and Dryden believed that English grammar was inferior to that of Latin or other foreign languages. They didn't follow some of the grammar rules we swear by.

Writers were of the opinion that French and Latin were much better languages for writing than English. Written English was very different from spoken English, and this can be considered a period of turmoil in English grammar.

In 1755, Dr Samuel Johnson came up with the Dictionary of the English Language, which helped to set the rules for Standard English Grammar. "The English Grammar Adapted to the Different Classes of Learners" released in 1795 by Lindley Murray further standardized English grammar rules.

John Dryden

John Milton

William Shakespeare

# THE JOURNEY OF YOGURT

🎓 **THE FIRST SPELLING TO BE RECORDED** was "yoghurd." It traveled in from the Turkish dictionary around the early 1600s. Soon, the word transformed into yogourt, yahourt, yaghourt, yogurd, yoghourt, yooghort, yughard, yoghurt, yohourth. Phew!

But it was the commercial use of the spelling "yogurt" that gave the final verdict. The dropping of the crucial "h" wasn't well received by traditionalists. They frowned at the audacity of the manufacturers and retailers who went ahead with the tweaked spelling.

This tiny storm in the market was mentioned in "The Grocer," the food industry's trade journal, and that too in a letter to the editor written in 2009 by Clair Cheney, Director General of the Provision Trade Federation. The letter said, "Isn't it time for The Grocer to catch up with the fact that the industry has long since dropped the "h" from yoghurt?"

Commenting on this heated debate, writer and etymologist Michael Quinion said, "It (yogurt) is more crisp and short, the word is spelt as it sounds." That meant it was a more phonetically correct version than yoghurt.

## FAST FACT...

📖 **A COMPENDIOUS DICTIONARY** of the English Language first released by Noah Webster in 1806 also has a new edition released annually, and is the commonly accepted American Dictionary.

Noah Webster

ANGLES

Saxons

JUTES

PIE

DUKE OF
NORMANDY

DOOMSDAY BOOK

VIKINGS

BEOWULF

SHAKESPEARE

501 ARCHAISM

↓

# Grammar through the Ages ←

KENNINGS

THORN

GEOFFREY CHAUCER

YOGH

THE CANTERBURY TALES

# ARRIVAL OF THE WEST GERMANICS

**THE ARRIVAL** of the West Germanic people in Britannia in the 5th century is often seen as the starting point of English Grammar. The West Germanics were mainly the Angles, Saxons, and the Jutes, who all spoke relatively similar versions of West Germanic. West Germanic itself was a version or kind of the ancient Germanic.

It was an ambitious Celtic warlord, namely Vortigern, who invited Hengest and Horsa, the Jutish brothers from Jutland, to defend the east coast of Britain against sea raids by the Picts. They were given permission to settle in the southern areas of Kent, Hampshire and the Isle of Wight in return. Soon, other Germanic tribes began undertaking the short journey across the North Sea, such as The Angles from the Angeln region who settled in large numbers on the east coast of Britain and the war-like Saxons from the Lower Saxony of Germany who infiltrated the southern part of mainland Britain. The Frisians, who were settled earlier in the marshes and islands of western Germany as well as Northern Holland, also began encroaching on the British mainland from 450 A.D. onwards. Soon these tribes began displacing the native Celts and established permanent settlements.

Their variations of Western Germanic were similar to modern Frisian and close enough to each other to be mutually intelligible.

## 130 FAST FACT...

📖 **FRISIAN WORDS LIKE**
"bûter" which became butter,
"boat" which stayed boat, and
"stoarm" that became storm
were added into English.

## 131 FAST FACT...

📖 **THE EUROPEAN** Invaders
were called "barbarians" by the
Celts, and they called the Celts
"weales" meaning "slaves" or
"foreigners," and from there
came the name "Wales."

## 129 FAST FACT...

📖 **THE LANGUAGE** that is
spoken in the Angeln region
in Germany shows great
resemblance to the English
spoken about 1,000 years
ago and even today can be
recognized as similar to English.

## 132 FAST FACT...

📖 **HENGEST AND HORSA**
mean "stallion" and "horse"
respectively and Horsa
was killed during the Battle
of Vortigen.

# MOTHER OF ALL LANGUAGES

**HERE'S AN INTERESTING** theory about the origin of languages. The existence of common words and features among many languages of Europe, India, and Asia caused scholars to believe that all languages have originated from one source, namely Proto-Indo European (PIE). PIE is believed to have been spoken four to six thousand years ago by a tribe that lived between the Black Sea and the Caspian Sea.

This language was never written down and its structure has been conjectured by modern linguists, who worked backwards from the hundreds or more languages that have descended from it in Europe and India. Sir William Jones began the work of reconstructing Proto-Indo-European in Bengal in the 1780s. He was the first one to recognize the links between Latin, Greek, and Sanskrit.

## FAST FACT...

**THE WORD** "pater," meaning father, is considered to be Proto-Indo European. That is the exact same word for father in both Latin and Greek. In Spanish, it is "padre" and in Sanskrit, "pita," both very close to the original word they are believed to have originated from.

## FAST FACT...

📖 **THE 4500-YEARS**-old Silk Route is considered to be the single most influential entity that resulted in the birth of proto-Indo European language, commonly called the ancestor of the Indo-European language.

## FAST FACT...

📖 **LITHUANIAN** is believed to be the closest language today to the Proto-Indo European language.

## FAST FACT...

📖 **WILLIAM JONES** was a hyperpolyglot who is believed to have known 13 languages thoroughly and another 28 reasonably well.

William Jones

## FAST FACT...

📖 **NAMES OF LOTS** of places ending in "-ing" meaning people of "(e.g. Worthing)" or "-ton" meaning village "(e.g. Burton)" or "-ford" meaning river crossing "(e.g. Ashford)" point at Anglo-Saxon settlements.

## FAST FACT...

📖 **IN NORSE**, the word "Viking" actually means "a pirate raid."

## FAST FACT...

📖 **IN 793**, the wealthy monastery at Lindisfarne in Northumbria was looted and sacked before the Vikings turned to invade south.

## FAST FACT...

📖 **ONLY ABOUT** 150 Norse words appeared in the manuscripts of the Old English period. Many more got added to the language over the next few centuries, finally reaching 1,000.

# THE VIKINGS

**THE SCANDINAVIAN** settlement started with the sporadic invasion of the east coast of Britain. They came from Denmark, Sweden, and Norway but the Danes came down most ferociously. The Vikings were ruthless; they plundered and piled the towns as well as monasteries of Northern England. By the 850s, they began raiding the southern parts of Britain and soon they started a full blown invasion to win over the entire country.

Alfred the Great finally checked this Viking expansion in 878 with the help of a treaty between the Anglo-Saxons and the Vikings, establishing the Danelaw. It roughly split the country into two halves along a line between London and Chester. The Vikings got the north and eastern parts and the Anglo-Saxons, the south and western. The Danelaw lasted less than a century but its great influences can be seen by the large number of places named with suffixes like "-by," "-gate," "-kirk," "-toft," etc. (e.g. Whitby, Grimsby, Ormskirk, Lowestoft, etc.). Also influenced were family names as seen many ending with "-son" (e.g. Johnson, Harrison, etc.)

The Vikings spoke an early Germanic language, Old Norse, which was similar to that spoken by the Anglo-Saxons. It is similar to modern day Icelandic, and it heavily influenced accents and pronunciations in northern England. It gradually merged with Old English and many Scandinavian terms were imported. About 1,000 Norse words have been added to the English vocabulary. Some commonly known words are bag, gap, knife, die, flat, etc. Also, English adopted Norse grammatical forms such as pronouns like "they," "them," and "their" eventually.

## FAST FACT...

📖 **THE TRANSITION** of Old English to Middle English is marked by the invasion of the island of Britain by the Duke of Normandy from Northern France in 1066.

## FAST FACT...

📖 **THE BOOK** in which William the Conqueror took stock of his new kingdom was called "Doomsday Book," and was specially written in Latin to emphasize its legal authority.

## FAST FACT...

📖 **THE VERY WORD** "Norman" comes from the word "Norsemen," showing how Vikings were descendants of the Anglo-Saxons.

## FAST FACT...

📖 **THE NORMANS** had abandoned Old Norse and begun speaking French. They spoke a rural dialect of French that had considerable amounts of German influences. The language was called Anglo-Norman or Norman French.

## FAST FACT...

📖 **THE NORMANS** gave English over 10,000 words, including those with suffixes such as -ment, -ity, and -tion, and prefixes such as con-, de-, ex-, trans-, and pre-.

William - The Conqueror

## 148 BEOWULF

**ONLY ABOUT 400** Anglo-Saxon texts survive today. The most well-known is the long epic poem, "Beowulf." It survives in only one manuscript called the "Nowell Codex."

The author/authors of this poem remain unknown, but it is believed that the poem was mostly written in the 8th century and then revised again in the 10th or 11th century. Set in Scandinavia, the poem's 3,182 lines illustrate how Old English was already a well-developed poetic language by that time.

Even in those early years, a large variety and depth of English vocabulary is seen in this poem, and a liking for synonyms and subtleties in meanings is very obvious. The poem uses 36 different words for hero, 20 different ones for man, 12 different terms to describe battle, and 11 for ship. There are some very attractive allusive compound words, or kennings as they are called, in this work of art such as "hronrad" (meaning whale-road or sea) or "banhus" (meaning bone-house literally or body). The poem was first printed in 1815 in Thorkelin.

## 149 FAST FACT...

**BEOWULF** has 903 compound nouns used in it, of which 578 are used only once and 518 are unique to it.

## 150 FAST FACT...

**THE MANUSCRIPT** of Beowulf is said to have got slightly burnt when a fire broke out in the building it was stored in. Evidence of this is the charred end on the top left.

# OLD ENGLISH'S CONTRIBUTIONS TO TODAY'S LEXICON

**WHEN THE WEST** Germanic tribes settled in England, it led to the mingling of their West Germanic and the English language. A large number of words imported from there into English. Some examples are "froast" (frost), "see" (sea), "miel" (meal), etc.

Latin brought in by missionaries was still used only by the elite few during the Old English period, so its influence on English was largely restricted to Church, dignitaries, and ceremonies. It gave us words like "priest," "vicar," "altar," "mass," "bishop," and "pope".

Many of the basic words used in Modern English have their roots in Old English, such as "earth", "house", "food", "drink", "sleep", "sing", "night", etc. It is amusing to know that a number of swear words that we commonly use today are of Anglo-Saxon origin!

Some of the most common and fundamental words we use today have come to us from the Old Norse language spoken by the Vikings. Under this list are words like smile, hug, call, cast, clip, die, flat, meek, sly, wrong, loose, happy, awkward, weak, worse, low, etc.

## FAST FACT...

**ABOUT 85%** of the approximately 30,000 Anglo-Saxon words found in texts and scriptures have gradually died out.

## FAST FACT...

**MOST OF THE** important "function" words such as but, in, at, to, from, and, etc. were all Anglo-Saxon words.

## 154 THE ROMAN INVASION

**IT WAS UNDER EMPEROR** Claudius that the Romans were able to defeat the ferocious British Celts and begin permanent occupation of Britain in 43 A.D.

The Romans faced a number of uprisings at the hands of the natives, such as Queen Boudicca in 61 A.D., but they managed to keep Britain as a part of itself for almost 400 years. This legacy was in the form of 200 "loanwords" that were coined by their soldiers and merchants. Some of these words were win (wine), caese (cheese), candel (candle), rosa (rose), cest (chest), and so on. It is important to note though that after a few centuries during the rise of The English Renaissance, Latin showed great influence on the language.

The use of Latin during the Roman rule was more or less confined to the nobility and ruling class as well as the inhabitants of the cities and towns. It did not replace the Celtic language in Britain as it has done in Gaul. In 410 A.D., due to attacks at home from the Visigoths, Ostrogoths and Vandals, the Romans abandoned Britain and completed this withdrawal by 436 A.D. fully.

### 155 FAST FACT...

**THE FIRST** time the Roman's entered Britain was in 55 B.C., under the great Julius Caesar.

### 156 FAST FACT...

**AFTER THE** withdrawal of the Romans from Britain, the language, and Britain, were said to have settled into the Dark Ages.

# CELTIC MYTHOLOGY

**CELTS SUCH** as the Gauls and Celtiberians, who were in close contact with Ancient Rome, lost their mythology during the Roman Empire. It led to their conversion to Christianity and the loss of their Celtic languages. But their mythology has been preserved through contemporary Roman and Christian sources. The Celts left very rudimentary remains of their ancestral mythologies in the form of written works during the Middle Ages.

Although the motif of God Lugh is found very consistently throughout the Celtic World, Celtic religion was characterized by great variations in local practices as they were not unified. Inscriptions of around 300 "genii locorum" or local deities have survived and been equated to their Roman counterparts.

What we know about Celtic religion and mythology is through archeology and not literature. It is believed that the Romans destroyed most of the Celtic writings and, in "De Bello," Giaco Caesar attested the fact that the Gaulish were literate but their priests were forbidden from writing and recording certain significant religious verses.

# ÆLFRIC'S DE TEMPORIBUS ANNI

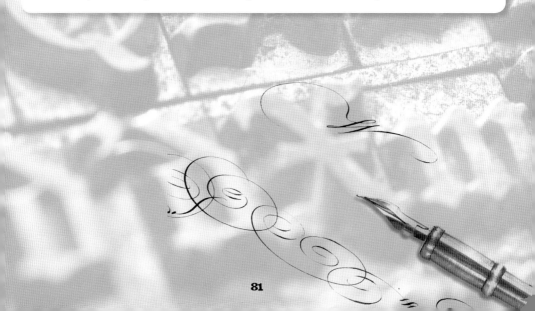 **AELFRIC'S** De Temporibus Anni was written by Aelfric of Eynsham, who according to great historian Peter Hunter Blair, a specialist in Anglo-Saxon history, was "a man comparable both in the quantity of his writings and in the quality of his mind even with Bede himself." Ælfric of Eynsham lived from 955 to 1010 A.D. Saint Bede is widely revered as the "Father of English History." Ælfric of Eynsham was an English abbot known to be one of the greatest Old English writers, who wrote in various genres including biblical commentaries, hagiography, and homilies.

"De Temporibus Anni" is a revolutionary handbook of the period. And even though its title is in Latin, it was written by Ælfric in the 10th century in Old English, which was the vernacular language in most parts of Western Europe. Being the first concise handbook of its kind in Old English, it was about calendar and computes, astronomy and natural science. It differed from the earlier works of Bede and Isidore in the language of its writing. Initially, the fact that De Temporibus Anni was written by Ælfric was unknown. It was only later on that he was credited for this first of a kind literary work in Old English.

De Temporibus Anni, which gave the layman a basic understanding of the relation between nature and time, encouraged other writers to write about complex subjects in vernacular Old English rather than only in Latin. This helped Old English literature and grammar flourish in this period.

# NORSE MYTHOLOGY

**NORSE MYTHOLOGY** is the mythology of the North Germanic people, primarily the Vikings of Denmark, Norway, Sweden, Iceland, Faroe Island, and Greenland. It is associated with paganism that was practised by the Norse people of those times. It involves the tales of God, Goddesses, beings, and superheroes.

Several medieval manuscripts of the Old English period are among the chief sources of information about Norse Mythology. Some of these include "Prose Edda by Snorri Starluson" in the 13th century and "Poetic Edda," also composed during that period. North Germanic languages such as Old Norse were used in these literary works. However, as new Scandinavian languages such as English evolved, the grammar of these new languages was inspired by these works, and a lot of words from Old Norse found their way into English grammar.

According to Norse mythology, the one eyed God, Odin, was the chief source and propagator of knowledge across different worlds. He was the ruler of Asgard and chief of the Aesir Gods. He introduced mankind to the runic alphabet. The various letters used in Old English, which included some of the Anglo Saxon rune letters like "thorn (þ)," originated from the runes in Old Norse.

## FAST FACT

📖 **"THOR,"** a God in Norse mythology has been popularized in modern times thanks to Marvel Comics, which have a series based on "Thor." There is also a Hollywood film about him.

82

## KENNINGS BY OLD ENGLISH "WORD-FISHERS!"

**A "KENNING"** is an extremely compressed form of a metaphor which formed a part of Anglo-Saxon and Norse poetry. It went on to become a common feature in a lot of poems written in English.

Kennings are used to make an indirect reference to an object by making use of a two word phrase, like "whale-road" was used to refer to the sea. A kenning for a spider would be "web-maker."

Interestingly, though kennings have been used in poetry since the Old English period itself, the word "kenning" was only coined in the 19th century. It is derived from the Old Norse word "kenna" which means to "know, recognize, perceive, feel, show, and teach." Kennings can be categorized in several different ways. They can be divided into simple and complex kennings.

## FAST FACT

**KENNINGS FIRST** appeared in the English language in Norse poetry and Anglo Saxon poetry. The epic poem, "Beowulf" is full of kennings.

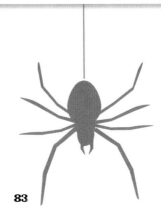

# KING ARTHUR – THE ONCE AND FUTURE KING

**CELTIC MYTHOLOGY** is deeply centered on the huge number of stories about the life, rule, conquests, and battles of King Arthur. He was a legendary British ruler who lived in the late 5th and early 6th centuries. There are a lot of literary works and folklore about his exploits against the Saxons that have been impossible for historians to confirm up to now.

In the 15th century, Sir Thomas Malory came up with a literary work called "Le Morte d'Arthur." From then on, King Arthur and his knights have been a part of numerous literary works.

The version of King Arthur that we know today is a composite collection of legends as narrated by different writers down the ages. When Celtic literature bloomed in the 11th century, Geoffrey of Monmouth transformed King Arthur into a superhero. By the time of King Henry VII, King Arthur's legend was well-established, and kings tried to emulate him. He was further glorified in the Victorian Era.

King Henry VII

King Arthur, his wife Guinevere, and his sword Excalibur were a part of Geoffrey's works. Lancelot and the Holy Grail were added to the legend after the works of the 12th century French writer, Chetien de Troyes. His "Knights of the Round Table" also appeared in works of this period. Arthurian literature dominated the Old English period.

## FAST FACT...

**KING ARTHUR** was also known as "The One, True King of the Britons."

## FAST FACT...

**THE BATTLE** of Camlann was his last battle in which he was killed.

# RELIGIOUS REFERENCES OF CHRISTIANITY AND JESUS

🎓 **THERE WAS A LOT OF OLD** English poetry that was religious in nature in most cases with references to Christianity and Jesus being made in them. The deofol is also seen to appear in Old English texts which later on became "the devil" in Modern English.

The major reason for the religious references of Christianity and Jesus in Old English works was the conversion of Anglo Saxons to Christianity. Old English poets began writing vernacular and didactic poetry with religious subjects. As such, this poetry can be divided into three broad categories – Biblical Poetry, Poems about Christ, and Saints' lives.

There were four major poetic manuscripts or literature codices in Old English, namely the "Caedmon" or "Junius" manuscript – an illustrated collection of poems on biblical narratives, the "Exeter Book" – an anthology of famous poems like Christ I, Christ II, and Christ III, the "Vercelli Book," and "Nowell Codex" (also called the Beowulf manuscript) .

Poems like Christ I and Christ II talk about Jesus, his life, and his baptism, and are purely religious poems which characterized the literature of that time.

# THE USE OF THE LETTER THORN

**THE OXFORD DICTIONARY** defines "thorn" as the letter, þ or Þ, representing the dental fricatives /ð/ and /θ/. It was eventually superseded by the digraph "th." Apart from being a letter in the dialects of Old English, Icelandic and Old Norse, it was also commonly found in some dialects of Middle English. The thorn was derived from an Old English runic alphabet called "Futhark."

During the Old English period, thorn was used commonly for writing English, just like eth (ð). However, unlike eth, thorn continued to be used even in the period of Middle English. An example of a sentence with the use of a thorn in it is "Wel gay wat zþis gome gered in grene." This is a sentence from Middle English. The word "þis" with a thorn would be written as "this" in Modern English.

By the 14th century, thorn started to become obsolete because Gothic style scripting made the letters "y" and thorn look very similar.

## FAST FACT

**FRENCH PRINTING** presses did not have the letter thorn. So they began to conveniently replace it with a "y." So 'Ye' in most cases is actually to be pronounced as "The!"

# THE USE OF LETTER "YOGH"

🎓 **YOGH WAS ANOTHER** letter that was used in Middle English but was among the 12 letters that did not make it to Modern English. The Oxford Dictionary defines yogh as "a Middle English letter (ʒ) used mainly where modern English has "gh and y." It was derived from the Old English form of the letter "g."

The yogh which was written as "ʒ" was pronounced as a throaty noise such as the "ch" in "Mach." Since the English language was not standardized at the time, there was quite a lot of confusion over the manner in which the Yogh was to be written, and the upper case and lower case forms of the letter looked almost similar with the lower case form only being smaller in form as compared to the upper case form of the letter.

The letter Yogh did not make it to Modern English because Norman and French scribes were completely against non-Latin characters coming into English. So, Yogh was replaced with the digraph "gh." Even so, the different types of pronunciations were elaborated, which can be clearly seen in the following three words-"cough," "taught," and "though." These words are spelled in the same manner in Modern English as well.

Yogh was replaced with "gh" very slowly, and it was only by the end of the 15th century that the use of yogh became obsolete. Hence, yogh, like thorn, died a natural death!

## FAST FACT

📖 **AMPERSAND**, ethel, wynn, and eng were other letters that didn't make it to Modern English.

# CHANGE IN GRAMMAR FROM OLD ENGLISH TO MIDDLE ENGLISH

🎓 **THE NORMAN** conquest of England was chiefly responsible for the birth and development of Middle English.

The conquest resulted in Norman speaking rulers and their subjects replacing English speaking political hierarchies. Thus, Norman soon became the language used in literature and polite discourse while Latin was used for administrative purposes.

It was only from the late 1200s that the influence of Norman began to be seen distinctly in English, and Middle English began to become characteristically different from Old English.

Several new words like "pork" for pig, "poultry" for chicken, "beef" for cow, "mutton" for sheep, and "honorable" for worthy came up in Middle English.

Words like court, judge, jury, appeal, and parliament are all of Anglo-Norman origin, and came into Middle English during this period. They have continued to be a part of Modern English as well.

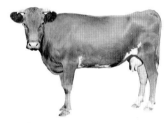

## 173 FAST FACT

📖 **MARGERY KEMPE** dictated the first autobiography written in English. It was called the "Book of Margery Kempe," and tells the story of her visions.

## 174 FAST FACT

📖 **MIDDLE ENGLISH** was heavily influenced by three languages – Latin, Scandinavian, and French.

# THE BOOK OF TALIESEN

🎓 **THE BOOK OF TALIESEN** is one of the oldest and most famous Welsh manuscripts. In Welsh, it is referred to as Llyfr Taliesin, a name given by Edward Lhuyd. It has a set of 56 poems written by the poet Taliesin.

The original manuscript also contains a few hymns and a collection of elegies to famous personalities like Dylan Eil Ton who is a character in the Welsh mythic "Mabinogion tales." Famous poems such as "The Battle of Trees" and "The Spoils of Annwfn" also formed a part of the manuscript.

The works in "The Book of Taliesen" are influenced partly by Latin texts, Christian texts and partly by Welsh and native British tradition. The original manuscript is known as "Peniarth MS 2" and is kept in the National Library of Wales. The entire manuscript was the work of a single scribe who is believed to have lived in Glamorgan.

# THE BOOK OF THE DUCHESS

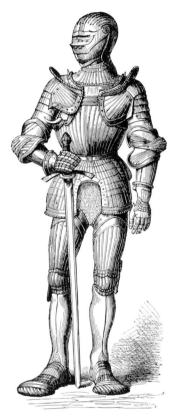

🎓 **ONE OF THE EARLIEST** and most legendary poems written by Geoffrey Chaucer was "The Book of the Duchess." It's believed to have been written somewhere between 1368 and 1372. It is also referred to as "The Death of Blaunche". Evidence suggests that this book was written in memory of Blanche of Lancaster on the request of her husband, John of Gaunt who was the earl of Richmond. There are several indirect references that have been made throughout the poem which suggest this.

The poem starts off with the sleepless poet lying in bed reading a book which is a collection of short stories. He reads the story of Ceyx and Alcone. The poet then goes to sleep and narrates his dream.

In his dream, he walks through a chamber with windows depicting the tale of Troy and the story of "The Romance of the Rose." He then follows a small dog into the forest where he finds out that Octavian of Rome is hunting. There, he sees a black knight composing a song for his dead lady. Throughout the remaining poem, the knight tries to indirectly explain to the poet that his wife is dead but the poet doesn't understand until he finally states it explicitly. The poet understands, and his dream and the poem come to an end.

# THE CANTERBURY TALES

👆 **THE CANTERBURY TALES ARE ARGUABLY** the most critically acclaimed works of the legendary late 14th century poet, Geoffrey Chaucer. It was a set of 24 tales narrated by the different protagonists of the work.

The greatest contribution that this work has made to English is the use of vernacular English instead of French and Latin. The Canterbury Tales is written in Middle English. The most appealing part of it is the variation in the structure and content of each different tale.

Chaucer's work is among the last written with the letter "e" being pronounced at the end of words like "fare" was pronounced with the phonetic pronunciation of "e" at the end. This word required pronunciation of words exactly the way they were spelt.

The Canterbury Tales is considered a Modern English masterpiece.

## FAST FACT

📖 **EACH OF CHAUCER'S** characters in Canterbury tales possess different views on reality. Chaucer worked very hard to ensure that no one story was better than the others.

# THE FATHER OF ENGLISH LITERATURE

**GEOFFREY CHAUCER IS KNOWN** as the "Father of English Literature." He is also often referred to as the savior of the Middle English language, which was threatened by French and Latin during that period due to the prevalent political situation. Serving as a bureaucrat, diplomat, and courtier, Chaucer is responsible for great developments in English grammar. In contrast to the alliterative Anglo-Saxon meter, Chaucer's works were an example of the continental accentual-syllabic meter which developed from the 12th century onwards.

Chaucer is also credited for having invented the rhyme royal which is a rhyme pattern, which goes a-b-a-b-b-c-c. In course of time, this became a standard rhyme form which was used by the poets of the time. He was also responsible for the standardization of the London dialect of Middle English. He used several Middle English words which although believed to be a common part of colloquial language of the times, were never used as a part of earlier writings. Some of these words were alkali, arbitration, amble, approaching, annex, etc.

His works weren't influenced by "The Great Vowel Shift." The House of Fame, The Book of Duchess, and The Canterbury Tales are among his greatest works.

Geoffrey Chaucer

## FAST FACT

**DURING THE HUNDRED YEARS** War, Geoffrey Chaucer was a prisoner of war. He was released by France after the ransom was paid.

## FAST FACT

**CHAUCER HAS** a crater on the far side of the moon named after him.

# ARCHAISM – STOP BEING OLD FASHIONED!

**THE OXFORD DICTIONARY** defines archaism as "(of a word or a style of language) no longer in everyday use, but sometimes used to impart an old-fashioned flavor." English happens to be a language which continues to undergo immense evolution, with new words coming into the dictionaries, and the style of speech and writing changing rapidly. All of us make use of archaic elements at some point in time.

Archaic elements still form a part of specific jargon in fields such as law, poetry, and geography, as well as religious texts. Archaisms are of two types – literary and lexical. Literary archaisms are often used in literary pieces deliberately, in order to make use of the style of older speech and writing. Since it involves archaic elements not in common use, it is written to be an attractive proposition for readers. For instance, "the whole creation groaneth and travaileth in pain together"—Iris Murdoch, 1987. Lexical archaisms on the other hand include words that are no longer in common use. E.g. Jeepers, crumbs, etc.

## FAST FACT

**SOME INTERESTING** archaic words that you should know are grumpish, crapulous, jargogle, twattle, gorgonize, cockalorum and jollux!

Archaisms are also categorized based on the periods in which they were in common use. E.g. Archaisms from the Victorian and Edwardian Era include luncheon, guv'nor, confound you, damnable cheek, etc. Archaic elements are used to evoke emotional attachments to the glorious ages of the past in many cases, like Iran is sometimes called Persia, which was its former name. Lawyers are the main culprits when it comes to indulging in archaism, using words like thereof, thereby, etc., in all legal writings.

# SHAKESPEARE AND HIS ENGLISH!

**WILLIAM SHAKESPEARE** (1564-1616) is widely regarded as the greatest English playwright of all times. His plays like Hamlet-Prince of Denmark, Merchant of Venice, and Julius Caesar, among a dozen, continue to captivate the imagination of people across the globe. They also continue to be read in his original writing style, which is different from both Middle English as well as Modern English.

Shakespearean English is considered to be a separate section of the English language altogether. Shakespeare used artistic licenses and the flexible nature of English in his times to come up with many words, and tweaked meanings of commonly used words to suit situations.

Richard II

Shakespeare changed nouns to verbs, verbs into adjectives, created new words by connecting existing ones or adding prefixes and suffixes, and devised wholly original words as well!

Over 500 English phrases in common use even today are credited to him, like "foul play" and "a sorry sight." English grammar truly owes a lot to him.

## FAST FACT

**AFTER THE WRITERS** of the Bible, Shakespeare is the second most quoted writer in the English language.

## FAST FACT

**RICHARD II** and King John are the only two Shakespearean plays that were written entirely in verse.

# YE OLDE ENGLISH

**🎓 "YE OLDE" IS A COMMONLY** used cliché believed to belong to Early Modern English of the 16th and 17th centuries. This cliché is commonly used in Great Britain even today.

The origin of "Ye Olde" and other words starting with "Ye" is credited to the gradual transition from the early Middle English alphabet (þ) to the digraph "th" used in Modern English. In the medieval English alphabet representation commonly used especially by the printing presses, the letter thorn (þ), which was pronounced as "th" and the letter "y" looked very similar. As a result, in numerous cases, they looked quite identical and were often substituted by printing presses and while writing for each other, purely by mistake. Once the use of the thorn became less common and there was a switch to the use of the digraph "th," this mistake stopped being repeated. The English of the earlier times then often came to be known as "Ye Olde" English and the cliché was born during the Early Modern English period.

Ye Olde English varies from Modern English greatly in many aspects of the English grammar used. The usage of pronouns is quite different, with "thou" being used for you and "thy" being used for your. The vocabulary and orthographic conventions are also quite different.

## FAST FACT

**📖 IN MODERN TIMES,** "Ye Olde" is often used to make fun of English supporters in sports.

## ENGLISH-LEGALESE

**THERE IS A SPECIALIZED VARIETY** of English used for legal documentation by lawyers, which is quite archaic in nature and differs greatly from commonly spoken English. David Mellinkoff in his book "The Language of the Law," written in 1963, has noted that legal English includes "distinctive words, meanings, phrases, and modes of expression."

## FAST FACT

**IN THE WORLD OF LAW,** it is widely believed that for a lawyer to have an in depth knowledge of law and learn Legalese, he needs to study Latin or/and French as well.

Legal English includes the usage of phrases and words that seem difficult and peculiar in comparison to commonly spoken English. Additionally, the writing conventions of legal English are quite different with the structures of sentences being different, uncommon pronouns being used (the aforesaid, the same, etc.), foreign phrases being used instead of English phrases (e.g. prima facie), insufficient punctuation usage and the usage of legal doublets (e.g. null and void).

One of the reasons responsible for these complications is the trilingual nature of law documentation during the Middle Ages. While law books were originally written in Latin, there was a shift to French in the 13th century, and finally, English became the language of law books. To avoid any confusion, lawyers simply started using both such words together. Hence legal doublets came into existence (cease and desist, fit and proper, etc).

Legal English is also referred to as legalese or lawspeak, and lawyers undergo extensive training to understand, speak, read, and write legalese.

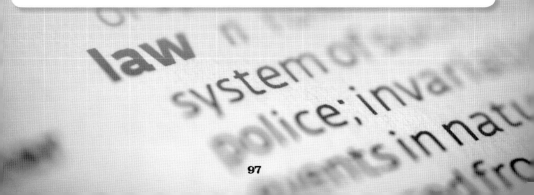

# ELIZABETHAN ENGLISH

**ELIZABETHAN ENGLISH REFERS** to the English and the laws of English grammar that existed during the period of the reign of Queen Elizabeth I, who was the Queen of England and Ireland from 1558 to 1603. It was an age of renaissance in English language and literature which corresponded with the period of the greatest English playwright of all times – William Shakespeare.

The plays in Elizabethan era had an influential effect on the spoken English of the times. The Elizabethans considered the sound of the language more important than logic. There was no concept of superlatives with words like "more" and "most" being used as intensifiers just like "very" is used today.

The inventive usage of words and the introduction of puns also took place during this period. For example, in "Julius Caesar" by Shakespeare, one of the characters, Cassius, puns on "Rome" and "room," which were pronounced alike. Terms like "What on earth" and "little wonder" became a part of English grammar through the plays of Shakespeare, which were filled with them.

Statue of Queen Elizabeth

Elizabethan pronunciations are quite different from those of Modern English due to English being in the process of the "Great Vowel Shift." So words like "love" and "prove" which do not seem to rhyme today actually rhymed perfectly back then. Over 4,000 new words were created during the Elizabethan era!

## FAST FACT

**THE ELIZABETHAN ALPHABET** had 24 letters, unlike the present day alphabet, which has 26 letters. "u" and "v", "i" and "j" were the same letter.

## FAST FACT

**MANY WORDS** that belonged to Elizabethan English are now extinct. One of them is "gong" which meant "dung."

4d

ARTIST UNKNOWN *c.*1575 / HARRISON

SPELLING

Non-rhotic

RHYMING SLANG

ALLUS

PYGMALION

NOWT

YORKSHIRE

ACCENTS

LABOV

501

AMERICAN SOUTH

# English Around the World

PIDGIN      HINGLISH

ESPERANTO      GULLAH

QUEEN'S ENGLISH

# MUCH ADO ABOUT SPELLING

**IT'S NOT TOO TOUGH TO SPOT** the differences between American English and the various languages it draws from. "Traveller" becomes "traveler", "analyse" becomes "analyze," "pretence" becomes "pretense," "centre" becomes "center," and "colour" becomes "color." Some of these have gradually evolved, while others have been brought about deliberately to reflect the spoken language of the people who used it.

Noah Webster had the objective of reforming spellings in mind when he wrote "An American Dictionary of the English Language," recording the spelling changes. A teacher himself, he also published what is now known as the "Blue-Backed Speller" in 1783. It was a part of a three-volume work to simplify English in American schools.

Differences in language are ultimately not just about grammar or spelling, but also about personal and national identity. For a newly-minted nation, it was one of the crucial ways in which to assert its identity in the eyes of the world.

## FAST FACT

**HENRY DAVID THOREAU** echoed Webster when he said, "When I read some of the rules for speaking and writing the English language correctly, I think any fool can make a rule, and every fool will mind it."

## FAST FACT

**INCIDENTALLY, THE ENGLISH WORD** "alphabet" is made by combining "alpha" and "beta," the first two letters of the Greek alphabet.

$$A \; B \; \Gamma \; \Delta \; E \; Z \; H \; \Theta$$
$$I \; K \; \Lambda \; M \; N \; \Xi \; O \; \Pi$$
$$P \; \Sigma \; T \; Y \; \Phi \; X \; \Psi \; \Omega$$

$$\alpha \; \beta \; \gamma \; \delta \; \epsilon \; \zeta \; \eta \; \theta$$
$$\iota \; \kappa \; \lambda \; \mu \; \nu \; \xi \; o \; \pi$$
$$\varsigma \; \sigma \; \tau \; \upsilon \; \varphi \; \chi \; \psi \; \omega$$

Greek Alphabets

# IT'S ALL GREEK AND LATIN TO ME!

🎓 **IT'S NO SECRET THAT TRACES** of the two classical languages are easily found in the roots, prefixes, and suffixes of several English words. In fact, at one point, students of English literature were expected to learn Latin and study the classics of Greece and Rome before starting on English writers.

The word "logos" or "logia" in Greek meaning "the study of a subject" provides the suffix for the English terms biology, etymology, sociology, astrology, and the like. Meanwhile, "phone" and "telephone" share the root Greek word "phone" meaning voice.

Latin finds its way into irregular plurals too. "Data" is actually a singular noun, and its plural is datum. "Analysis," originally a Greek addition, becomes analyses.

Meanwhile, words from Latin like "focus" turn to "foci" while "larva" turns to larvae. The suffix "–rix" was borrowed from Latin to convert singular feminine nouns to plural. Words like "administratix" and "aviatrix' were common earlier, but are now being replaced by "–ess."

Emperor Julius Caesar

## FAST FACT

📖 **THE ENGLISH LANGUAGE** is written in the Roman script, which was derived from the Greek system of writing.

## FAST FACT

📖 **EVEN SHAKESPEARE** felt that Greek was incomprehensible in his time! A passage in Julius Caesar has a character speaking Greek which a listener could not understand, and said, "It was Greek to me."

# COUNTRY COUSINS!

🎓 **IT'S A POPULAR FEELING THAT EVERYTHING** sounds smarter with an English accent. But which English accent are they talking about? There are several English dialects and accents in England.

One of the most famous ones would be the Cockney accent, popularized by the movie "My Fair Lady." Cockney-speaking Eliza Doolittle's attempts to improve her language were mined for jokes at her expense.

## FAST FACT

📖 **COCKNEY IS "NON-RHOTIC"** in its articulation, meaning that the "r" sound will only be produced in a limited sense.

## FAST FACT

📖 **COCKNEY RHYMING** Slang evolved to be difficult to decipher for outsiders, possibly to escape detection by officials or to invoke a sense of identity for speakers and to keep others out.

29 USA — BROADWAY MUSICAL — MY FAIR LADY

The songs in the productions feature several classic phonological (sound based) examples of Cockney pronunciation and grammar, illustrating its difference from the Queen's English in RP, for example, the dropping of the "h" sound at the beginning of words – "ouse" for "house," and adding it in front of other words that begin with vowels. These days, however, Cockney is one of the more popular dialects in England, famous for its "Cockney rhyming slang."

How does it go? You take a word and find a replacement word or phrase for it that rhymes with it but is not similar to it. So telephone, which rhymes with dog and bone becomes bone. "He never picks up the bone/Get off the dog and bone!" It sounds simple enough, but ends up with entertaining results, like stairs become apples and pears, as in when Britney Spears stands for beers!

## FAST FACT

📖 **MY FAIR LADY WAS** an adaptation of a play called "Pygmalion," written by George Bernard Shaw.

БЕРНАРД ШО

NR BULGAR

POSTA

## FAST FACT

📖 **MULTIPLE HUGO** Award-winning fantasy author China Mieville was named "China" (China plate to rhyme with '"mate," or friend) in true Cockney rhyming slang style.

## FAST FACT

📖 **COCKNEY SPEECH** is associated with the East End of London. Traditionally, to be called Cockney, one had to be born in an area where the tolling bells of St. Mary le Bow church could be heard.

# THA CAN ALLUS TELL A YORKSHIREMAN!

**...BUT YOU CAN'T TELL HIM MUCH.** If you're not from Yorkshire and that didn't make much sense, don't worry. We've deciphered it for you. "Allus" means "always" and "tell" stands for identify, not speak to. An old saying about Yorkshire people, it also draws attention to their distinctive way of speaking.

Located in the North of England, the Yorkshire dialect retains traces of Anglo-Saxon, Norman, and Germanic influences in its speech. Words that reflect its Norse origins that are also commonly used in English include dale (valley), lug (to pull), and reckon (to think over). Other words like nowt (nothing), summat (something), and owt (anything) are unique to it.

One of the most noticeable grammatical features of Yorkshire English is the use of "tha" and "thee" as distinct second person pronouns, something that has faded from the modern forms of English grammar.

Yorkshire dialect uses "tha" and "thee" to indicate the subject and object form of "you" even today, though its use in speech varies from speaker to speaker.

For example, "Where have you been?" could be said in a Yorkshire dialect as "Where have tha been?" or "I'll help you" could be said as "'I'll help thee."

## FAST FACT

📖 **YORKSHIRE,** its dialect, and accents feature in classics of English literature like "Wuthering Heights" by Emily Bronte, "The Secret Garden" by Frances Hodgson Burnett, and many of James Herriot's novels like "Vet in Harness" and "All Creatures Great and Small."

## FAST FACT

📖 **THE "U" SOUND** in "but", "bus", "put", and "butter" are traditionally pronounced the same way in a Yorkshire accent. It is similar to the "oo" sound as pronounced in "stood."

## FAST FACT

📖 **THE "H" SOUND** that occurs in words like has and have is often dropped. "I'll help thee" could be pronounced "I'll elp thee." "Where have tha been" could even become "where 'avetha bin," since vowels like the long "ee" in been are typically shortened.

# AMERICAN ACCENTS

🎓 **THE AMERICAN ACCENT HAS BEEN** a coveted one ever since America cemented its status as a world superpower, making it a prestigous accent. Linguists have identified certain accents that command respect over others for social and political reasons.

Within America, there are several accents with greater and lesser prestige, with several people attempting to make their accents sound closer to the prestige accent. William Labov studied this in his famous "New York Department Store Study" in 1972.

Labov picked up data from salespeople in department stores by simply asking them for directions to the "fourth floor" of the store. He chose the "fourth floor" because of the presence of the "r" sound, the pronunciation of which can indicate which accent is closest to the dominant prestige class. In speech, one might not pronounce the "r" sound in "fourth" but articulate the final "r" sound.

Labov then went to three stores. He found that salespeople in Sak's (with well-off clientele) rolled their r's most. The staff at the more middle-class Macy's rolled their Rs more when they were asked to repeat themselves, showing that they were conscious of imitating the prestige dialect!

## FAST FACT

📖 **THE AMERICAN SOUTH** also provides some of its most well-known dialects and accents. Those fond of using "y'all" (the contracted second-person pronoun used to refer to you all or all of you) would testify to that. The sound "I" is also pronounced as "ah", as in "ah am going home."

## 212 FAST FACT

📖 **STEPHEN FRY** has said that "It only takes a room full of Americans for the English and the Australians to realize how much we have in common."

## 213 FAST FACT

📖 **EX-PRESIDENT BILL CLINTON** speaks with a Southern drawl, George Bush with a Texas twang, and Barack Obama with a little bit of a Chicagoan accent.

## 214 FAST FACT

📖 **BOSTON BRAHMINS** are known for their distinctive accents, as are the residents of the South Appalachian mountains.

## WHEN TWO WORLDS MEET

**AT ITS PEAK, IT WAS SAID** that the sun never set on the British Empire. Rumored to span across almost one-fourth of the globe, the English empire grew with the spread of trade and conquest. What the colonizers had never anticipated was the changes they brought in the languages around the world as a result of the contact between cultures.

A "pidgin" is a language that came into being as a result of interaction between two language groups whose speakers have no other language in common. There were several English-based "pidgins" of which a few, like Chinese Pidgin English, West African Pidgin English, and Cameroon Pidgin English are known and documented. Some of them are even in use today as creoles, since children acquire these languages from the speech community around them.

The English language has gained a lot from this exchange, with several words entering its lexicon. The phrase "chop-chop" is said to have its origins in Chinese Pidgin English, meaning "hurry" or "move fast." The word "wiki" in Wikipedia has its roots in a Hawaiian word meaning fast and quick, and there are several other words whose etymologies show their pidgin history.

## FAST FACT

**SCHOLARS HAVE** speculated that the word "pidgin" comes from the Chinese pronunciation of the English word "business." However, there is no strong evidence for this claim.

## PARDON MY HINGLISH

**HINGLISH IS A WIDELY SPOKEN VARIETY** of English, spoken by Hindi and English speakers across the world. Hindi speakers were exposed to English on a large scale during British trade and rule in India, and as a result began to learn both languages side by side.

As is the case when any two languages lead a parallel existence, there is a fair amount of borrowing between the two. English is a both prestige language and a second language for a number of Hindi speakers, and the continuous co-existence of the two has led to a large amount of intermixing that is known as Hinglish!

Lexical borrowings, that is, at the level of grammatical structure are also frequent. Hinglish words sometimes feature Hindi nouns with English plural suffixes, generally "s" for example, "dabbas"(dabba means food container).

Suffixes are also borrowed into English. He's a filmwallah or a theaterwallah, with "wallah" being a Hindi noun suffix meaning "one who is employed in the profession of."

## FAST FACT

**HINDI AND ENGLISH** are the official languages of India. There is no selected national language of the union.

# TALK PIDGIN!

**NO ONE QUITE KNOWS HOW HUMAN LANGUAGE** evolved, and the forms it currently exists in. The study of pidgins and creoles is therefore much more fascinating, because it provides a living example of the ways in which human languages grow and adapt.

While pidgins developed as a means of communication, creoles are another form of language that have evolved as a result of contact. Creoles are spoken natively by people, while pidgins remain in use for some time and fade out.

## FAST FACT

📖 **GULLAH IS ANOTHER** creole that draws on English. It was initially spoken by slaves of African-American origin who were made to work on American plantations.

Linguist,
**L. L. Zamenhof**

Scholars argue that creoles developed as a result of pidgins becoming native languages for speakers over a period of time. Tok Pisin, for example, is a creole spoken in Papua New Guinea that derives its name from "Talk Pidgin" in English! It has elements of English. Some Papua New Guineans speak it as a first, and others as a second language.

Some of its pronouns are similar to English ones – "mi," "yu," and "em," for "I," "you," "he/she," and "it" and others – "mipela," "yupela," and "ol" for "plural" pronouns "we," "you," and "all" are different. Fruit is called "pikininibilongdiwai" or "prut," which is similar to English phonetically. "Bot" stands for "Boat" in Tok-Pisin, and "banana boat" stands for a commercial or trading vessel! This probably reflects the trading associations from which the term originated.

## FAST FACT

📖 **ESPERANTO WAS** an attempt to construct or create a common world language using linguistic features from various language groups.

## 222 HER MAJESTY'S VOICE

**THE QUEEN'S ENGLISH,** contrary to popular perception, is not based on the way the current reigning monarch speaks. The "Queen's English" today is a standardized form of the English language with emphasis on accent, vocabulary, grammar, and style to set it apart from other regional variations and dialects.

In contemporary times the Queen's English is most likely to be associated with an "RP" accent, which stands for Received Pronunciation. It was widely held to be "proper" English, and the most suitable way of speaking it. In the 19th century, this accent was initially spoken in parts of south-east England. It soon came to be seen as a mark of distinction and prestige for members of the upper classes and acquired other speakers across the country aspiring for this status.

What's interesting is that unlike most accents, RP was not a feature of the region the speaker was from; it embodied where the speaker studied or worked. As this was most likely to be prestigious public schools, offices of the Church, the judiciary, Parliament, or the Civil Services, speaking the Queen's English soon came to suggest a person from a good family, with good education, and well-placed in the professional world.

Meanwhile, English speakers in England largely prefer to retain their local accents and dialects today, with broadcasters also following the same policy.

## 223 FAST FACT

**THE LANGUAGE** is named after the gender of the monarch in power; we know it as the Queen's English but the concept of the King's English also exists.

## L'OCEAN
prés d'Europe,
auec les Costes de
FRANCE, d'ESPAGNE, de PORTUGAL,
d'ANGLETER.re de HOLANDE, de DANEM.re
Suivant les Cartes Marines
les plus Nouvelles
Par P. Du Val, Geogr. du Roy
1666.

NORWEGE

MER DE
DANEMARC

ESCOSSE

IRLANDE

MER
D'IR-
LANDE

ANGLETER

HOLANDE

FLANDRE

PICARDIE

NORMANDIE

BRETAGNE

FRAN

POICTOU

SAINTONGE

OCEAN

La Manche

MER DE FRANCE

OCCIDENTAL

Golfe de
Gascogne

GUIENNE

ou

ASTURIE

BISCAYE

CATALO-
GNE

MER DE

GALICE

ESPAGNE

VALENCE

PORTUGAL

POR-
TUGAL

MURCIE

ANDALOUSIE

GRENADE

de Gibraltar

Golfe des
Yeguas

ROYA.e de FEZ

BAR

MAROC

AFRI

E U R O

## FAST FACT

**📖 THE QUEEN'S ENGLISH**
spoken in England is often
confused with "BBC English,"
after the accents of the
newscasters. This is because
the BBC's first general
manager Lord Reith preferred
people who spoke RP accented
English, as it was believed to
be an accent free of dialects
and most intelligible to the
maximum number of people.

## FAST FACT

**📖 IN 2012 NEWSPAPERS**
reported the dissolution of the
40 year old Queen's English
Society, whose objectives included
educating the public in the
"correct and elegant usage" of
English. There's also an Anti-
Queen's English Society!

## FAST FACT

**📖 ACTORS STEPHEN FRY,** Hugh
Laurie, and Hugh Grant are known
for their RP English, while actors
like Ian McKellan, Patrick Stewart
adopt an RP-accent for roles.

Sir Ian McKellen

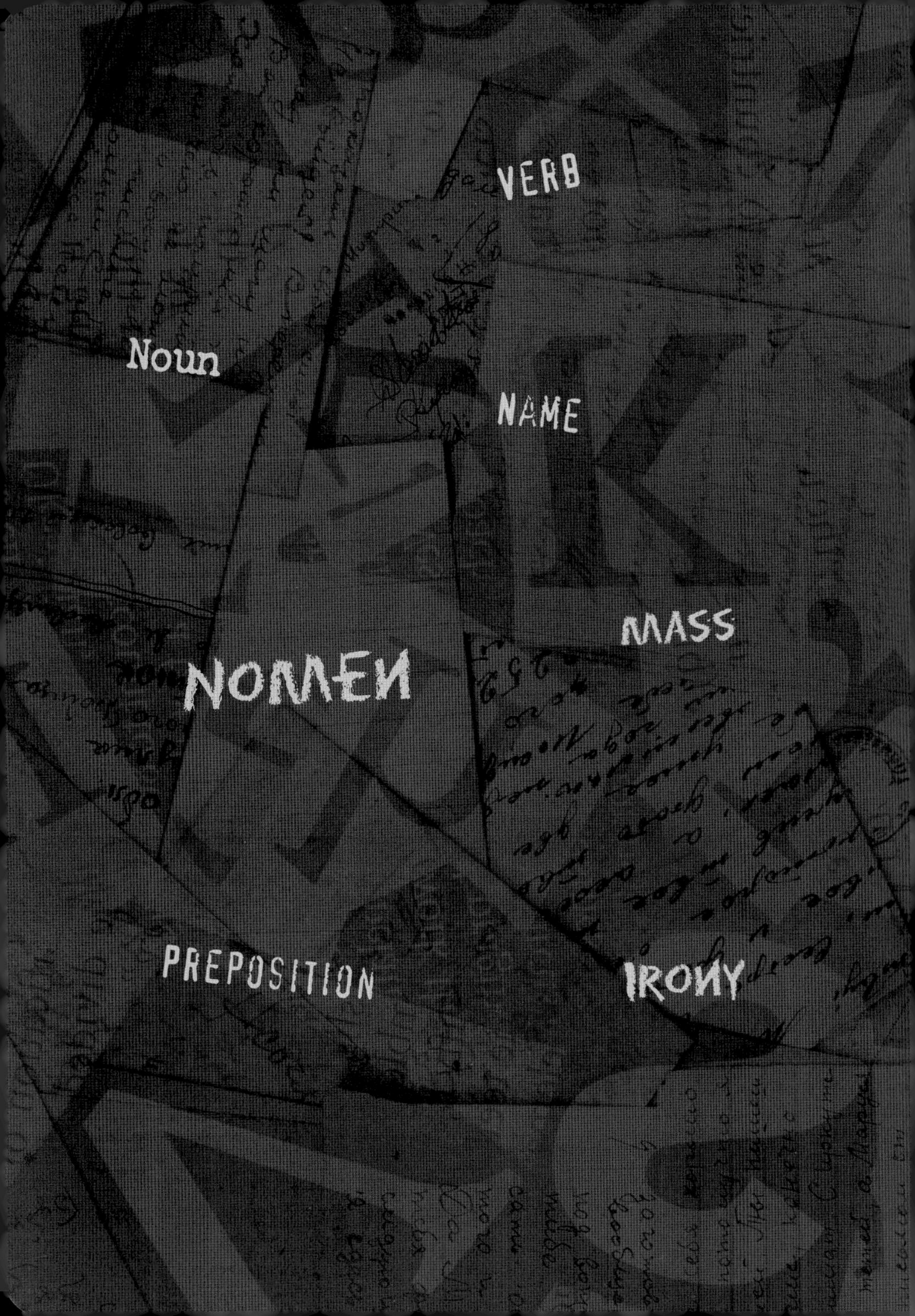

VERB

Noun

NAME

MASS

NOMEN

PREPOSITION

IRONY

# Parts of Speech

# MARRIAGE IS A VERB, NOT A NOUN...

🎓 **...SAID BARBARA DE ANGELIS,** indicating that it is something that involves action rather than description. Verbs are "action words," indicating what a person, object, or thing is, what it is doing, and what is occurring to it. Along with nouns, verbs are one of the key word classes in English.

The English language is one of many that follow the S-V-O order, which means that in any grammatically correct sentence spoken by any native of the language, the subject will come first, followed by the verb, and the object being referred to. For e.g., in English, we do not say "singing for the audience she is" when we mean that she is singing for the audience.

Even children learn the rules of their usage without being taught. Verbs in English carry some amount of inflection for tense, meaning that verbs change according to the tense. Babies start off by saying "Me want!" (or I want!), which is the infinitive or standard form of the verb. They tend to trip up on irregular verbs, which are verbs that are not inflected for tense in the same way. English has several irregular verbs, and they end up saying "I goed" before gradually moving on to "I went" or "I am going!"

It's a while before children pick up on the process of "verbing," or making verbs out of nouns. If you like "Facebooking" or "dialoging," you're in on the secret!

## FAST FACT...

📖 **OTHER LANGUAGES** that follow the S-V-O order are Yoruba, Portuguese, Greek, and Spanish. S-V-O (subject-verb-object) structured languages include Hungarian, Tamil, and Persian.

# WHAT'S IN A NAME?

**A NOUN** is a word that names a person, place, action, thing, or quality. English has several categories of nouns; proper nouns, common nouns, concrete, and abstract nouns.

A school of thought represented by linguist Benjamin Whorf believed that categories of our language (like nouns) influence how we see the world. For e.g., the grammatical distinction between common nouns and proper nouns could shape our cognitive representation of these concepts. We have very specific nouns denoting personhood – "a girl," "a man," (not "one of a male human") but fewer forms for words like "rice," "air," or "electricity." Whorf suggested that these distinctions in the language could shape our perception of these things in existence, individualizing some things, and seeing others as units when they are also made up of individual units.

In English, the plural form of the word is marked on the noun. Researchers have found that even children as small as four years old acquire the linguistic rules of marking plurals on nouns. Children were tested with made-up words like "wug," and found that they could apply a grammatical rule - adding the "s" sound without being taught. Other rules of plural include adding the suffixes "es," "ies," "ves" in addition to other irregular forms.

At the end of the day, a rose by any other name would smell as sweet, but would sound really weird to say!

## FAST FACT...

📖 **THE NOUN** is, in fact, one of the first categories of grammar and speech that babies acquire as they learn language.

## FAST FACT...

📖 **"NOUN" COMES** from the Latin word "nomen," meaning name. A noun is a naming word.

## FAST FACT...

📖 **NOUN CLASSES** that cannot be counted are called "mass" or "uncountable nouns." They are used with definite articles.

# THIS IS THE SORT OF ENGLISH UP WITH WHICH I WILL NOT PUT...

**...HERE WINSTON CHURCHILL** is breaking one of the best known rules – you can't end sentences with a preposition. Turns out that rule can be ignored, unless you're a really strict grammarian. Saying "up is the direction in which I'm going" is quite a mouthful, so it's okay to use a preposition at the end of that sentence.

Preposition comes from a Latin word that means "to put in front of." Prepositions are placed before the nouns or pronouns they connect, to the rest of the sentence. "She is good to us" connects us to the adjective "good." The word following the preposition becomes the object of the sentence.

Prepositions seem small, but are the glue that keeps sentences together because they indicate relations of place (on, at, or in), direction (off, to, into), time (at, on, in for, before, after), agent (by), and reason (from, for) between things.

You can also combine a preposition and a verb (or a verb and an adverb) to form a phrasal verb. "Boil down" and "aim at" are good examples. Some phrasal verbs have become such well-known expressions that they are fixed and do not take any other form. They are also often used as nouns when two are merged to form one word or phrase. "Bailout," a word that has been in the news a lot recently is one such word, as are "makeup" and "standby."

Winston Churchill

## FAST FACT...

📖 **IF YOU'RE** learning English as a foreign language, prepositions can be tough! The same word can be used to refer to different things.

## FAST FACT...

📖 **COLLOQUIALLY**, adding the preposition "at" at the end of questions has become popular in American English, with phrases like "where you at," meaning where are you becoming very popular.

## FAST FACT...

📖 **WORDS LIKE** "afore," "ere," (meaning before) and "betwixt" (meaning between) are all prepositions that have fallen out of use, except in poetry or literature.

# IRONY

**BOTH IRONY** and euphemisms are forms of speech that indirectly communicate their message. Irony is the less gentle of the two, where one thing is said, but its appearance, contrast, absence, or even opposite is indicated, but not explicitly referred to.

Irony derives its meaning from a Greek comic character called the "eiron." The eiron was a character who acted less smart than he was and spoke in a restrained manner. In the play, the eiron eventually triumphs over the alazon, who is an arrogant and bragging figure.

There are different degrees of irony in literature. There's verbal irony where a sentence's meaning is different than the words in it; Mark Twain's statement "The reports of my death have greatly been exaggerated" is presumably an ironic referral to the press's misreporting of his death when he was very much alive.

Situational irony, as the name suggests, is when the arrangement of a situation throws up its irony for the characters or the plot. For e.g., a student is punished for copying by being made to copy the lines a thousand times. Dramatic irony seeps through work, where the reader or viewers are aware of information that characters are not, and can see what is coming before the characters can.

## FAST FACT...

**A REAL-LIFE** example of situational irony is Orson Welles' radio broadcast of the play "War of the Worlds." Several listeners who tuned into the middle of the play overheard an announcement about Martians invading New York and, unaware that it was a dramatic production, fled from their houses!

# METAPHOR

**A METAPHOR** is a figure of speech that brings together two ideas that are unlike each other, based on a common quality. As a linguistic and cognitive tool, metaphors make it possible for us to broaden the scope of our communication. They are related to our abstract reasoning abilities and capacity for analogy.

Conventional metaphors are the most commonly used form of metaphors. Whether you think life is a race or a road or a journey, you would agree that expressing that abstract thought in a metaphor makes it easier to put it in words.

Creative metaphors are original or new combinations – Raymond Chandler called Los Angeles "a city with all the personality of a paper cup," while mixed metaphors combine two or more metaphors without any point of similarity, and come up with unfortunate results. Watch out for these – you could start out for the course but end up on a sticky wicket.

## FAST FACT...

**SCHOLARS** have classified more than 10 types of metaphors, including dead metaphors (metaphors that have been overused and don't have the same effect) and visual metaphors (where an image invokes an implied connection).

## FAST FACT...

**BOOK** and movie titles are also retrospectively used as metaphors – that's a "Catch 22 situation," "This is such a 1984ish nightmare" or "it's a Cinderella story."

## FAST FACT...

**POET WALLACE STEVENS** felt that "reality is a cliché from which we escape by metaphor."

# WHAT YOU HEAR IS WHAT YOU GET

**MANY GRAMMARIANS** believe that the process of onomatopoeia – words formed in the imitation of sounds – was the basis of evolution of words in the human language. Human beings coined words out of exclamations they made, or heard animals and birds make, or came across in their environment. This theory has been pooh-poohed by others who cite the fact that there are very few words in most human languages that are onomatopoeic in nature.

Linguists have pointed out that the relationship between words and their meaning are arbitrary; i.e., the word "table" doesn't resemble in spelling or sound like an actual table. As a figure of speech, onomatopoeia performs the useful function of bringing meanings of words closer to the sounds they make. When we're stuck for words, we tend to fall back on gestures or miming sounds. "It made that click sound" or the door went "creeeaaakkkk, it really freaked me out."

## FAST FACT...

**ALL LANGUAGES** have onomatopoeic words, but funnily enough, they are not the same! In English, the sound of laughter is written as hahaha or heehee, French captures it as héhéhé, and Portuguese is hahaha and huehuehue.

## FAST FACT...

**THE COMMODITY** "zip" is named after the sound it makes.

## FAST FACT...

**WORDS THAT** begin with plosives – the sound made by the letters b, p, t – are used to communicate loud noises and sounds because of the impact they make.

# OXYMORON

**OF ALL THE FIGURES OF SPEECH,** the oxymoron has to inherently be the funniest. The word "oxymoron" is in itself an oxymoron! It's derived from the Greek words "oxus," which means sharp and "moros," meaning dull.

An oxymoron is a figure of speech that combines two or more contradictory phrases that, in sum, express an important relation. Can you hear the deafening silence at that? If so, act natural.

Oxymora (plural of oxymoron) are of different classes. Some unintentional ones like "almost exactly," "eloquent silence," and "random order" are direct oxymora since the contradiction is evident from the literal meaning of the words.

Most oxymora are intentionally used to invoke laughter, though they can be deeply philosophical as well. Ask people who see the glass as half full. From Heraclitus' "Nothing is permanent, except change" to Wilde's "I can resist everything except temptation," oxymora help us look at the world in a whole new way.

## PACKING A PUN-CH

🎓 **"IT WAS HOW** she made a living, but it made life not worth living" is a classic example of a pun. Puns rely on the gap between the sound and meaning of a word, and turn it to their advantage.

Puns are often called the lowest form of humor because of their reliance on manipulating the sound of words for effect. These are homophones, where the pun is created by replacing one word with another similar sounding one. For example "Old kings never die, they're just throne away."

Then there are homographic puns that substitute similar sounding but differently spelled words, as in "Did you hear about the Italian chef? He pasta way."

**NO Two Weighs About It !**

## FAST FACT...

📖 **A FREUDIAN** slip is said to be a statement where you say one thing but mean your mother. Gotcha!

Sigmund Freud

127

## FAST FACT

📖 **PUN-DIT AMBROSE** Pierce said a pun was "a form of wit, to which wise men stoop and fools aspire."

## FAST FACT

📖 **ANOTHER DEFENDER** of puns was Jonathan Swift, who even wrote a piece called "The Art of Punning."

## FAST FACT

📖 **A POPULAR** form of punning is the Tom Swifty, named after a series of books with the same name. The Tom Swift books regularly featured adverbial puns – "He can't be that innocent" said Tom naively.

## AS EXPRESSIVE AS A SIMILE

**A SIMILE** compares one object or set of relations to another using the words "like" or "as" to connect the two. As a figure of speech, it draws a comparison without stating the obvious or literal facts. While a metaphor states that the two units are similar, a simile, as an analogy, expresses their similarity or likeness in comparative terms.

Take the case of animal similes that have been popular for a long time. Bats aren't really blind, though people still say that so-and-so is blind as a bat, while it seems unlikely that there's been a bull in a china shop recently. Some of them hit the nail on the head though.

By keeping two things side by side, similes help us describe some of the incommunicable parts of our experience. Perhaps the most similes we know have to do with love, which has variously been described as a red rose, a wild flower, the sun, a flame... the list is long.

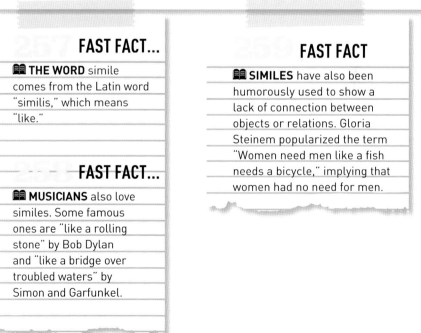

### FAST FACT...

**THE WORD** simile comes from the Latin word "similis," which means "like."

### FAST FACT...

**MUSICIANS** also love similes. Some famous ones are "like a rolling stone" by Bob Dylan and "like a bridge over troubled waters" by Simon and Garfunkel.

### FAST FACT

**SIMILES** have also been humorously used to show a lack of connection between objects or relations. Gloria Steinem popularized the term "Women need men like a fish needs a bicycle," implying that women had no need for men.

## ALMOST HUMAN

**EMILY DICKINSON** famously wrote "Because I could not stop for Death/He kindly stopped for me." In personification, objects or relations are given a human quality and inanimate entities are given characteristics of living things.

The tendency to personify non-human things is an old one, and humans have projected humans features onto forces of nature, animals, birds, and ideas.

Nature remains a personification favorite, with poets and writers across the ages personifying aspects of nature. Wordsworth's famous poem "Daffodils" starting with "I wandered lonely as a cloud" is a classic example.

Similarly, "love is blind," "fame is fickle", or "time heals all wounds", are all examples of the personification of abstract ideas.

## FAST FACT

**AESOP'S FABLES** and Grimm's Fairy Tales are full of examples of personification because they have characters like Godfather Death, The Devil and his Grandmother while Aesop's Fables features contests between the Wind and the Sun.

📖 **SHAKESPEARE** too was a master of personification – "O time, thou must untangle this, not I. It is too hard a knot for me t'untie."

📖 **COUNTRIES** and regions are frequently personified – England is Britannica while the American government is embodied in Uncle Sam.

📖 **IN THE EARLY** days of mechanical technology, people feared that machines had "a mind of their own," which reflects their personification.

HERE IS NO DARKNESS BUT IGNORANCE

## TELL ME MORE

**MARK TWAIN'S** advice to writers was "when you catch an adjective, kill it." He was speaking figuratively, but trying to make a point. One of the eight lexical categories of English, an adjective is a "describing word" that qualifies or describes a noun in terms of certain attributes – big, small, fat, or thin.

In the English language, nouns and verbs carry the grammatical number (or plural) and qualifiers are modified depending on the noun. For example, in English we would say "this train is full" and "these trains are full," never "these trains is fulls." In this case, the adjective remains the same, while in other languages, like French, it changes to "ce train est plein" "ces trains sont pleins."

Many linguists have pointed out that a language that does not grow or change is more likely to die. English has also changed and welcomed several new eponymous adjectives named after people or events over the years. Adjectives are part of the "open class" of words in English grammar. A "Newtonian" paradigm in physics instantly refers to the work of Isaac Newton, and the entire English language of a period has been described by the adjectives "Elizabethan" and "Shakespearean."

Mark Twain

## FAST FACT...

**GRAMMATICAL** plural is also a way to recognize most adjectives; if you can't make it plural by adding a suffix, it's likely to be an adjective!

## FAST FACT...

**THE WORDS** "good," "old," "new," and "great" are among the most popular adjectives in use in English.

## ON A HIGH

**A CLIMAX** is a figure of speech in which the meaning communicated rises with each word or phrase to reach a climax at the end of the sentence. Napoleon Hill's statement – "What the mind of man can conceive and believe, it can achieve," is an example. Rudyard Kipling's assertion in "If you can fill the unforgiving minute, with sixty seconds worth of distance run, yours is the Earth and all that's in it/ and, what's more, you'll be a Man, my son!" is an example of a climax, and a periodic sentence.

A periodic sentence is one where the meaning is not complete till the last word, which is where the climax in Julius Caesar's momentous utterance "Veni, Vedi, Vici" (I came, I saw, I conquered) is also one such phrase where a crescendo is reached at the last word.

An anticlimax is just the opposite, when the first phrases or clauses of a sentence build up a sentence, only to have its grandeur brought crashing down by the second half. "If you can't convince them, confuse them" is an example of an anticlimax, as is Mark Twain's tongue in cheek statement – "It is better to remain silent and be thought a fool than to open one's mouth and remove all doubt!"

## FAST FACT...

**THE WORD** climax comes from a Greek word meaning "ladder," describing the rise in degree of what is being communicated.

## FAST FACT...

**THE COMMON** quote about rejection that says "the first couple of years are hard, but then you get used to it" is an example of anticlimax.

## THE MISSING LINK

·····················································································

T **FACT IS**, a language wouldn't die without conjunctions. But they do make life easier. Conjunctions like and, or, nor, but, yet, soon, and for join separate words or phrases or parts of sentences into one unit.

One of the common myths in grammar is that you cannot begin sentences with because. The reason behind this is that in writing, people tend to supply only the subordinate clause and not the principal one. While the implied principal clause is clear when someone says "because I said so!" it's better to restructure your sentence to make sure the principal clause is clear!

### FAST FACT

📖 **A POPULAR ACRONYM** for the common conjunctions is FANBOYS, which stands for For, And, Nor, But, Or, Yet, Soon.

### FAST FACT

📖 **COMIC CHARACTER** Homer Simpson's "d'oh" is now well-known, as is the throaty "Zoinks!" from Scooby Doo's character Shaggy.

### FAST FACT

📖 **AY CARUMBA!** and olé are interjections of surprise and excitement, which have crossed over from Spanish.

# WHEN WORDS ARE NOT ENOUGH

**INTERJECTIONS** are not typically counted as words by linguists and grammarians, and they do not have any grammatical relation to the rest of the sentence they may appear with. They can also appear by themselves, and are typically followed by an exclamation mark.

Interjections can be purely sound based, like "Oh!," "Ah!," "Eek!," "Ha!," "Huh!," or "Aaah." However, they can also be formed with nouns, verbs, and adverbs, as in "Behold!," "Alas!," or "wow," and can be used to indicate lamentations, or calls for divine intervention.

Interjections from other languages are also regularly found in English, and are savored by those who use them! "Eureka!" is a famous Greek one, now even referred to as "a Eureka moment." Interjections are very popular with comic book writers, who probably had to innovate to fit characters' reactions into small frames.

While largely associated with speech, interjections also make appearances in print. Children's writer Enid Blyton peppered her books with "Crumbs!" and "golly!" both of which are now not in common use. American writers, meanwhile, popularized interjections like "gee," "yeah," (yes) and "no way" (exclaiming in surprise).

## FAST FACT

📖 **"YOICKS**!" is a common interjection used in hunting circles to urge foxes to run.

## FAST FACT

📖 **SOUNDS** like "er," "ah," and "umm" are also considered interjections and used widely in comics.

# NOT ALLOWED

**HOW TO SAY** no without hurting people is something grammar should teach us! Negation, or saying no, is a simple skill with all sorts of complicated ramifications. Why, a person who says no or declines too much can get a reputation for being too negative. However, grammar allows us plenty of ways of saying no without actually saying no. Sneaky, isn't it?

The standard form of negation in English grammar is the negative particle "not" or its contracted form "nt" added to an affirmative or declarative sentence. This is known as polarity, with the negation being marked as negative polarity on a standard affirmative sentence.

There are other ways of refusing people gently, by adding privative prefixes "un," "a," and "in" since they change the meaning of a word from positive to negative. For e.g., "I'm uninterested" or "that's ahistorical." Going with a double negative could buy you some breathing space without making an outright assertion, like "he's not unattractive." Got the point?

Other negative elements with a better reputation include pronouns like no-one, nobody, nothing, and adverbs like never and nowhere. Double negatives are frequently used in informal speech, as the Rolling Stones would say, "I can't get no satisfaction!"

## FAST FACT

**IN SIMPLE** negation, the negative particle "not" is added after the auxiliary or helping verb "is" (various form of the auxiliary verb "to be"), have, or do.

## FAST FACT

**THERE ARE** privative suffixes as well – harmless, graceless, or shameless are some examples.

## BETTY BOUGHT A BIT OF BUTTER

🎓 **HOW MUCH WOOD** could a wood-chuck chuck if a wood-chuck could chuck wood? This riddle is an example of both alliteration, a figure of speech in English, and assonance, a feature of sound in language. Alliteration is the repetition of similar consonantal sounds that occur at the beginning of the word, whether in a phrase or a number of words across a sentence.

Assonance is a feature similar to alliteration, except that in assonance, the vowel sound in adjacent words is repeated. In the first sentence, the "u" sound in "wood" and "could" is repeated.

Consonance, meanwhile, is the repetition of two or more consonants, broken by a vowel sound in between the two. Stick and stuck are examples of consonance.

A similar device popular in poetry is repetition, which takes many forms. A popular form is the "anaphora," which is the repletion of a single word or phrase. Mary Elizabeth Frye used this in the lines, "Do not stand at my grave and weep/I am not there/I do not sleep/ I am a thousand winds that blow."

## FAST FACT

📖 **CHILDREN'S** author Dr. Seuss used alliteration extensively in his poems because it's one of the best ways to teach children letters and sounds.

## FAST FACT

📖 **ANOTHER FAMOUS** use of alliteration can be found in Tintin Comics; Captain Haddock is known for saying "Thundering Typhoons!" and "Blistering Barnacles!"

## FAST FACT

📖 **JANE AUSTEN'S** novels Pride and Prejudice and Sense and Sensibility are both alliterative.

# HE SAID, SHE SAID

**WHILE ENGLISH** marks the class of biological sex with personal pronouns like he, she, his, and hers (note that this is sex, not gender), it also has a gender neutral or abstract form (it, its, they) for nouns.

Nouns that also denote professions do not originally carry any gender suffixes like "ette" or "elle," though certain nouns are seen as male or female by association. The dictionary definition of "waiter" uses the third person pronoun "one," and does not specify which gender the word is. The same is true for articles "a" and "the." French, for example has distinct articles like – le (male), la (female), l' (to form the singular of masculine and feminine plural words that begin with vowel sounds), and les (plural masculine and feminine form).

Many efforts are taken to make English a more gender-neutral language even with existing words. The usage of "actor" nowadays signifies both male and female, as does dancer, manager, and other related words.

## FAST FACT

📖 **THERE ARE** no masculine nouns for certain professions like maid or seamstress in English.

## FAST FACT

📖 **PERSONIFICATION** of certain nouns – like countries, for example, leads to them acquiring a gender; in their root form, they have no gender.

## FAST FACT

📖 **IN 2013, SWEDEN** introduced a gender neutral pronoun "hen" as a substitute for he or she.

# I'VE BEEN WAITING SINCE THE BEGINNING OF TIME!

**HYPERBOLE** is a figure of speech where relations between objects are represented in an exaggerated way for effect.

When a person is describing their love as one of the greatest of all time, or promising them the earth, the stars, and the moon with it, its an aggrandizement that is overlooked only because they happen to be in love. The desire to use hyperbole possibly vanishes after the love is gone too!

Julius Caesar

The other class of people that love using hyperbole are satirists. Jane Austen captures this in her book "Sense and Sensibility," when Elinor observes that "the sweetest girls in the world were to be met with in every part of England, under every possible variation or form, face, temper, and understanding," making it sound like England was overpopulated with sweet girls.

Julius Caesar was said to "bestride the narrow world like a Colossus," while Lady Macbeth feared that "all the perfumes of Arabia" would not be able to remove the guilt of her crime.

## FAST FACT

📖 **JONATHAN SWIFT** wrote "A Modest Proposal," in which he suggested that the poor in Ireland sell their children as food for money; needless to say, the idea was hyperbolic and intended satirically.

## FAST FACT

📖 **HYPERBOLE** is also used in politics to score points. The recent surveillance scam saw pundits comparing surveillance agencies to "Big Brother" in 1984, while opponents claimed that this was a hyperbolic claim.

# DON'T LOOK A GIFT HORSE IN THE MOUTH — NO, REALLY!

**THE THEORY** of transformational grammar holds that we can make an infinite number of sentences using very few and fixed rules of grammar.

Any language contains lots of idioms, which are phrases that carry figurative meanings if not literal meanings. You could call John a good egg, for e.g., and it would mean the same as "a good man." There is nothing wrong with the construction of the sentence. However, to many foreign language speakers, idioms like these seem meaningless, and the reverse is true as well. For e.g., when we say someone got an "A for effort," we do not literally mean that they have got the letter, and someone unfamiliar with the school system may not realize that "A"s are letter grades awarded for performance. Do we actually go back to square one to start over or cut to a chase when we're trying to be clearer?

## FAST FACT

**GRAMMARIANS** also point out that you can extend the sentence almost forever using the word "and." "John was a good man and a good friend and a great father, and he was also the kind of person who loved soccer, and he spent every Sunday playing with his friends..." it could go on. Really.

143

## FAST FACT

📖 **GRAMMARIANS** have talked about the syntagmatic axis of languages. The sentence "John is a good man" cannot be said as "John good man a is."

## FAST FACT

📖 **THE PARADIGMATIC** axis varies, as in idiomatic use. John is a good man, a bad man, and a dead man are all acceptable.

## FAST FACT

📖 **OTHER** common idioms are "bring the house down," and "take my hat off to."

*Keywords*

*Ranking*

*SEO*

*Analysis*

*Optimization*

# WHEN IN DOUBT

**PROVERBS LIKE** idioms help human speech move beyond its literal limits to more figurative domains. While idioms often have nouns and their modified forms as a source, proverbs draw on figures of speech like similes, metaphors, and hyperbole to get their meaning. They are also a source of meaning about existence or wisdom to guide action, like the proverb above. Its full form was either "do without" or "do nowt" (nothing).

Some are literal in their construction – one bad apple spoils the rest, blood is thicker than water or look before you leap – and can be easily understood if one knows the meaning of the constituent words. However, when we're talking about a quiet person who we don't know much about, the proverb "still waters run deep" should be seen figuratively.

Proverbs have also been modified for comic effect by playing on the literal and figurative meaning. The "paraprosdokian" is a figure of speech where the second half of a phrase ends unexpectedly, changing the meaning of the whole unit. Famous papradoskian proverbs include – when the going gets tough, the tough... go shopping.

A change in proverbs reflects a culture's changing values as well. While the proverbial ant's work ethic was held as model, people today are more likely to say "greed is good!"

## FAST FACT

📖 **"WHEN** I'm good, I'm very good, and when I'm bad I'm better" said Mae West, illustrating a papradoskian.

## FAST FACT

📖 **ANTI-PROVERBS** riff on well-known proverbs for humorous effect; he who laughs last laughs best because he probably just figured out the joke.

## FAST FACT

📖 **PROVERBS CAN** provide contradictory advice, so be careful! While the best things in life are free, there is also no such thing as a free lunch.

## FAST FACT

📖 **ANOTHER PROVERB** modification is a Wellerism, which manipulates the meaning of a proverb to show it cannot always be taken literally. "The pen is mightier than the sword," he said, vainly trying to cut the knot with his nib.

## FAST FACT

📖 **FRANKLIN ROOSEVELT** said that "we consider too much the good luck of the early bird and not enough the luck of the early worm."

# ADVERBIALLY YOURS

**ADVERBS ARE THE SUBJECT** of much discussion in the writers' community over the matter – are they good or not? "I am dead to adverbs; they cannot excite me...I cannot learn adverbs; and what is more, I won't", said Mark Twain.

Adverbs are a part of speech that modifies the meaning of a verb, an adjective or another adverb. An adverb is used to provide more information about the manner in which something is done – slowly, quickly, fairly. A rule of thumb to distinguish adverbs from adjectives – apply the question "how" to any sentence, and the adverb should give you the answer.

## FAST FACT

**A POPULAR** form of punning is the Tom Swifty, named after a series of books of the same name. The Tom Swift books regularly featured adverbial puns – "'He can't be that innocent', said Tom naively."

Linguists have identified what they call adverbial disjuncts where adverbs are added but they don't add any meaning to the sentence. For example, "Interestingly, I would never have considered the proposal last year" linguistically conveys the meaning that "I would never have considered the proposal interesting last year" rather than "it was interesting that I would never have considered the proposal last year."

Whether you like adverbs or hate them, we can't do without them. But make sure to use them carefully and wisely!

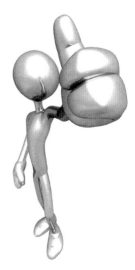

# ONE POTATO, TWO POTATOES

**THE MAJORITY** of plurals in English follow certain fixed rules – the suffices s, es, and z. For e.g., words that end with a vocalic sound or certain consonants add an s in the plural, though the sound is actually a "z." Words that end in the sounds made by p, t, k, and f also add an "s" to form the plural. However the pronunciation of this is "s" and not "z." Lastly, words that end in ch, jh or related sounds, add "es" to form the plural. This is pronounced as iz.

Plurals are also complicated by a whole lot of irregular nouns and verbs. There's a popular little poem going around that sums up these irregularities:

We'll begin with a box and the plural is boxes.
But the plural of ox should be oxen, not oxes.

Not all plurals are easy to figure out though. You're better off trying to toss a coin and guess!

## FAST FACT

**OTHER IRREGULAR** plurals include mouse (s) and mice (p), wife (s) and wives (p), story (s), stories (p), foot (s) and feet (p).

## FAST FACT

**PRONUNCIATIONS OF** words don't often follow the spelling while trying to follow plurals. Author T.S. Watt summed it up "Beware of heard, a dreadful word that looks like beard but sounds like bird."

# 308 ARTICLE OF INTEREST

**ARTICLES IN ENGLISH** grammar are not to be taken lightly; would you rather see "a blockbuster film that everyone is talking about" or "the blockbuster film that everyone is talking about?" The correct answer is both, of course.

A definite article is a word that tells you in more detail about the type of thing that is being referred to by the noun. "The" is used to indicate when something is one of a kind, a proper noun that is a name or something that is a member of a class of things.

"A" and "an" are indefinite articles, used when we do not or cannot specify the noun being referred to. It is also used to refer abstractly to a class of things, as in a day of sorrow, a pack of crows.

The article "an" is used for words beginning with vocalic sounds – like the first sound of "elephant," "an underground tunnel," etc. P.S. - watch out for the "h" sounds as in honor, or the "u" at the beginning of university! The "h" is silent, and the "u" is written as a vowel, but pronounced with the consonantal sound "yew" or "yoo." This rule causes some confusion, since these letters are not pronounced as they are written, so it's tricky to remember which article to use.

## 309 FAST FACT

**THE ARTICLES** "a" and "an" are derived from an older English version of the word "one."

## 310 FAST FACT

**"TEH"** is a common error made while typing the word "the" on a computer; it is now used as a noun!

FAMILY

Centum

SATEM

SANSKRIT

ENGLISH

LATIN

ORIGIN

AVATAR

# Sanskrit and English Grammar – the Connection ←

# FAMILY TREE

**THE STUDY OF LANGUAGE** is a fascinating subject, and the further back you go into a language's history, the more surprising it gets. English is no exception to this rule, being distantly related to several other languages in the world that are members of the Indo-European language family.

The discovery that English and Sanskrit had much in common, in spite of having little contact, stunned theorists. Surprised by the linguistic similarities between disparate languages, scholars began to hypothesize the existence of an ancient language called the "proto-Indo-European" language that would later give rise to the various branches of the Indo-European group.

Language historians now believe that the speakers of the Proto-Indo-European languages spread to different parts of the world. Their language (spoken between 4,000-6,000 years ago) changed with their travels, leading the original Proto-language to die out, but leaving several distinguishable elements in the languages that evolved later.

The Proto-Indo-European languages are divided into two branches – the "Centum" and the "Satem." The Italic languages (of which Latin is one), Hellenic (Greek), and West Germanic languages, like Old English, are all part of the Centum languages. Sanskrit, which is an Indic language and Persian, from the Iranian family, are also a part of this group. Several words from these languages share similarities in vocabulary – the Persian word for name is "naama," while the Latin word is "nom," and Sanskrit is "naaman."

Perhaps one day, the mystery of these languages will be explained fully. Till then, it remains an unsolved riddle in the history of an already captivating subject!

## FAST FACT

📖 **HISTORIANS COULDN'T** find any written evidence to prove the existence of the Proto-Indo-European language because writing was not much in use then.

## FAST FACT

📖 **THE CENTUM** and Satem distinction is also made on the basis of the sounds that characterize speech in the two languages.

## WELL I NEVER!

**JAMES CAMERON'S AVATAR** is only a recent example of a number of a word that has been borrowed into English or formed using a Sanskrit word. Words like "yoga," "nirvana," and "ashram" are commonly known, but the other connections between Sanskrit and English run deeper.

Many scholars feel that Sanskrit is in fact the "mother of all languages," even English. And it is true that the two languages have a surprising number of grammatical and phonemic similarities. These are largely to the influence of Latin, which has structurally influenced English.

William Jones, an ancient Indian scholar, studied Sanskrit, Greek, and Latin and felt that "both in the roots of verbs and the forms of grammar, than could possibly have been produced by accident; so strong indeed, that no philologer could examine them all three, without believing them to have sprung from some common source, which, perhaps, no longer exists." And later studies proved that linguistically.

It still doesn't prepare one for the surprise of seeing two such languages so far apart from each other sharing so many features. The words "mother" and "father," derived from the Latin "mater" and "pater" are similar to the Sanskrit "matra" and "pitra." The English "new" from the Latin "novus" resembles the Sanskrit "nav" or "nava." Other English words are borrowed from something, including names of animals. Shampoo, for instance, is said to have been derived from Sanskrit-origin "champior" massage!

## FAST FACT

📖 **SANSKRIT AND LATIN** (which has strongly influenced English structurally) are both classical languages in which the great literature, philosophy, and religious works of the age were written.

## FAST FACT

📖 **AN AVATAR** in Sanskrit refers to an incarnation of a God in one life.

## FAST FACT

📖 **THE WORDS CRIMSON,** cheetah, and aubergine are all of Sanskrit origin.

George Bernard Shaw

THEY

THEREIN

UNCOPYRIGHTABLE

MAY

PRONUNCIATION

THEY

HUNGRY

ANGRY

MIGHT

501

THEY

↓

# Fun Facts on English Grammar

QUEUE

↑

LITERALLY

PANGRAMS

## 318 "THEY" CAN BE ONE PERSON!

🎓 **IT IS QUITE** interesting to note that though "they" is commonly used to refer to more than one person or thing. To most of us, the use of "they" in singular form is grammatically incorrect. However, the usage of "they" to refer to a singular object is perfectly acceptable grammatically. In fact, "they" has been used to refer to singular objects since 600 years. When "they" is used in this form, it is referred to as "singular they."

The use of singular "they" and its inflected forms (like "them" and "their") typically occur in the following instances:

- When an individual person of an unknown gender is being referred to. This usage is commonly referred to as "epicene they." There has often been a lot of debate among grammar experts on how such people must be referred to in sentences. The use of singular "they" helps in sorting this problem. For e.g., I don't know who hit my dog, but "they" are surely in for a tough time.

- When an indeterminate number of objects is being referred to. When "they" is referred to in this form, it is also referred to as "generic they." In such cases, it is unknown as to whether "they" is being used in singular or in plural form. For e.g., anyone who thinks "they" have travel sickness, please take necessary precautions.

So remember, "they" stand corrected if they check you for using singular "they!"

## FAST FACT

📖 **THE LONGEST WORD** in the English language that is commonly used and does not contain any letter that is repeated is "uncopyrightable."

## FAST FACT

📖 **"QUEUEING" IS THE** only word in the English language with five consecutive vowels appearing in it.

## FAST FACT

📖 **THERE ARE NINE** smaller words that can be found in the word "therein" without changing the order of the letters. These are here, there, herein, her, in, rein, he, the, ere.

# 322 YOU HAVE "LITERALLY" NEVER USED THIS WORD CORRECTLY!

🎓 **THE OXFORD DICTIONARY DEFINES "LITERALLY"** as an adverb which means "in a literal manner or sense; exactly." This was the only definition of this word in the Oxford dictionary for a very long time. However, the common usage of "literally" in today's times is in a non-literal sense or exaggerated sense! For example,"You are literally as fast a lightning bolt!" Obviously, it is impossible to be that fast, which clearly shows that literally is being used in an exaggerated sense and, hence, goes against its primary definition in the Oxford dictionary.

In fact, in modern day spoken English, "literally" is being mistakenly used in place of the word "figuratively." The primary definition of the word "figuratively" in the Oxford dictionary is "departing from a literal use of words; metaphorical!" For example,"You are figuratively as fast as a lightning bolt!"

Thus, Modern English has resulted in the complete distortion of the word "literally" In fact, the misuse of the word "literally" is something that started in the beginning of the early 16th century itself. Poets and the playwrights of the time were responsible for this literary oddity as they made use of poetic liberties to use words in scenarios wherein they were actually not supposed to fit in grammatically. However, the misuse of the word "literally" only spiraled out of proportion in the late 20th century.

The misuse of this word resulted in the Oxford dictionary introducing a secondary definition for it which is "informal; used for emphasis while not being literally true."

## 323 FAST FACT

📖 **THE WORD "BOOKKEEPER"** (along with its verb form "bookkeeping") is the only unhyphenated English word that possesses three consecutive double letters.

## 324 FAST FACT

📖 **"R" IS THE MOST** commonly used consonant in English.

## 325 FAST FACT

📖 **"QUEUE" IS THE ONLY** word in the English language that doesn't change in pronunciation if the last four letters are removed!

# DON'T CALL ME "PANTS!"

**A VERY INTERESTING AND ASTOUNDING** fact that most of us would not have heard about is that the word "pants" was considered a bad word in England in the 1880s, and up to the early part of the 20th century, it was considered a word not worthy of gentleman! In England, "trousers" was believed to be the correct word that was to be used for an outer garment that was used to cover the body from the waist to the ankles. The word "pants" was often used in a derogatory sense. For example – you don't want a kick in the pants, do you?

In the United Kingdom and Ireland, "trousers" is a general term. The word "pants" is used to refer to underwear. In most parts of the world though, the word "pants" has come to be used in a more universal sense for all garments that cover the body from waist to ankle separately on both legs. So elastic garments or even silk garments of this type are referred to as "pants."

However, trousers are used to refer to formally worn garments of this type which have a waist-band, a fly-front, and belt-loops. Furthermore, "pants" are worn by both genders while "trousers" are worn by only males. Confused? So who wears the pants in your house?

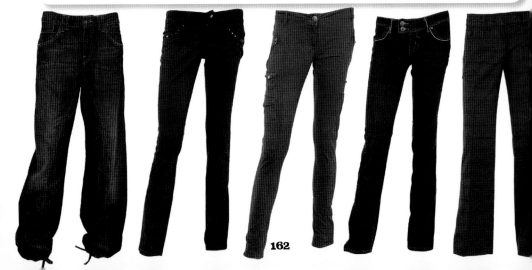

# FAST FACT

📖 **THE ONLY TWO WORDS** in the Oxford English Dictionary that end in "-gry" are "angry" and "hungry."

# FAST FACT

📖 **THE OLDEST WORD** in the Oxford English Dictionary that is still in common use is "town."

# FAST FACT

📖 **FORTY IS THE** only number in which the letters that form it appear in the order that they appear in the English alphabet.

# 330 THIS "MAY" HAPPEN BUT THAT "MIGHT" NOT!

**IT IS VERY COMMON TO INTERCHANGE** two words in English grammar that are similar in meaning. However, some of these pairs of words are to be used only in certain specific cases. A good example is the use of the words "may" and "might." We often interchange them as "I might come tomorrow morning" and "I may come tomorrow morning." But there is a big difference. When a person says "I might," it is supposed to imply far more uncertainty that when he says "I may."

Hence, the word "may" indicates a possibility while the word "might" indicates a very high level of uncertainty. To make sure that you use both of these words correctly, always keep in mind that the word "might" is supposed to be used when something is a "mighty long way" from actually taking place. Use the word "may" in all other cases.

Since English grammar is so full of exceptions for everything, we have to remember exceptions while using "may" and "might" as well! The word "might" is also the past tense of the word "may." So "might" has to be used in all cases when you refer to the past. Secondly, "may" must be used in cases where you seek permission. In such cases, might is not applicable. So, "may" we move on?

## FAST FACT

📖 **ONE IS THE ONLY** number in which the letters appear in the exact reverse order of their appearance in the English alphabet.

## FAST FACT

📖 **"FOUR" IS THE ONLY** word whose numerical value is equal to the number of letters in it!

## FAST FACT

📖 **"THE COMPLEX HOUSES** married and single soldiers and their families" is a grammatically correct sentence!

# PANGRAMS IN ENGLISH

🎓 **PANGRAMS IN ENGLISH ARE SENTENCES** that contain all the letters in the English alphabet in a single sentence itself. Pangrams are used for testing typefaces, testing equipment, and for developing skills such as typing on keyboards, typewriting, handwriting, and calligraphy. Pangrams which are short and coherent are very difficult to come by, as English grammar has 26 different letters, and some of these, such as "q" and "x," are not used very commonly.

There is only one pangram in English which is short and universally accepted for keyboard testing. A lot of us would have probably been made to write this sentence down multiple times as children when we were learning the art of writing from our primary school teachers. That pangram is – "The quick brown fox jumps over the lazy dog." We would have also seen this pangram when our computer displays different font samples. Computer programers are most well-acquainted with this pangram.

This pangram first appeared in "The Michigan School Moderator" in the 1885 issue of March 14th. It was suggested as a sentence that could be used for writing practice. In its original form, the pangram started with "a" and not "the." In later times though, the use of the word "the" to begin this pangram became very common.

Another pangram which can compare to this one in brevity and coherence, and has become popular in English recently is "The quick onyx goblin jumps over the lazy dwarf." Try coming up with one yourself!

## FAST FACT

 **SINCE YOU SPIT** while pronouncing the following letters, they are considered as germ spreaders – f, p, t, d, and s. Try using them less!

## FAST FACT

**THE MOST DIFFICULT** tongue twister in English is considered to be -"The sixth sick sheik's sixth sheep's sick."

## FAST FACT

 **IF YOU LOVE SCRABBLE,** "QUIXOTRY" is the word that will earn you maximum points.

## FAST FACT

 **ONE OF THE MOST** interesting facts about words in the English language is that the female form of all words in English are longer than their corresponding male forms, except for in one case. The word "widow" is an exception to this. Its male form "widower" is longer.

## "HOPEFULLY," YOU WILL USE THIS WORD CORRECTLY NEXT TIME!

**JUST LIKE THE WORD "LITERALLY,"** the word "hopefully" is also misused in most cases in Modern English. The primary definition for this word in the Oxford Dictionary is "in a hopeful way." In modern usage though, "hopefully" satisfies the meaning "it is to be hoped" rather than "in a hopeful way" like in the following sentence – "hopefully, we will have a holiday tomorrow." This is an incorrect form of this adverb's usage, and most of us are guilty of making the mistake at some point in time or the other!

The word "hopefully" is an adverb. The correct usage of an adverb is when it is used to modify a verb. Hence, the correct usage of "hopefully" would be in cases such as in the following sentences – "he prayed **hopefully** to God" and "he looked **hopefully** into the distance." A lot of other words like "apparently," "thankfully," "mercifully," and "sadly" are often used as adverbs in place of the word "hopefully" by writers as well as in common spoken English. As such, the use of "hopefully" as a pure adverb in Modern English has drastically reduced. Being an adverb, the word "hopefully" is not supposed to be used to start a sentence in most cases.

Just like in the case of the word "literally," when the Oxford dictionary lost all possible hope of people making use of the word "hopefully" correctly rather than as a sentence adverb, it added the second meaning as well. Poor Oxford!

THANKFULLY

MERCIFULLY

APPARENTLY

## 340 FAST FACT

📖 **MOST WORDS IN THE** Oxford English dictionary begin with the letter "s."

## 341 FAST FACT

📖 **SHEARS, TROUSERS,** and scissors are some of the words which do not have any singular form in the English language.

## 342 FAST FACT

📖 **"TYPEWRITER" IS THE** longest word that can be typed on a QWERTY keyboard by using letters that appear in a single row on the keyboard.

## 344 FAST FACT

📖 **THERE ARE ONLY** four words in the English language that end with the letters "dous." They are tremendous, horrendous, hazardous, and stupendous. The letters "dous" in the combination are among the most uncommon endings for English words.

## 343 FAST FACT

📖 **THERE IS ONLY ONE WORD** in English grammar that ends with the letters "mt," and that is "dreamt." Dreamt is the past tense form of the word "dream." Most of the other words of a similar type, like "scream" have the letters "ed" at the end in their past tense forms.

# STRANGE SENTENCES!

**PLEASE READ THE FOLLOWING SENTENCE** "Buffalo buffalo Buffalo buffalo buffalo buffalo Buffalo buffalo." Yes, it's a sentence and it's grammatically correct! The sentence mentioned above clearly shows how one word can be used to represent different parts of speech. This sentence was featured in Steve Pinker's 1994 book as an example of a sentence that may sound "nonsensical" but yet make perfect "grammatical sense."

The sentence makes use of the word "buffalo" in three different forms where it represents three different parts of speech. The word buffalo is repeated eight times in this sentence. It is used as a noun adjunct to refer to the city of Buffalo, New York, United States in the first, fourth, and seventh cases. It is used as a noun to refer to the animal, buffalo (also called bison in the United States of

America) in the second, fifth, and eighth cases. The word "buffalo" is used in its uncommon verb form in the third and the sixth cases to refer to the act of "bullying" or "intimidating." Keeping this in mind, try making sense of this sentence! It's much easier now.

The sentence means-
The buffalo from Buffalo who is buffaloed by buffalo from Buffalo, buffalo (verb form) other buffalo from Buffalo.
This sentence truly shows how English can be a funny language!

## 346 FAST FACT

📖 **ANOTHER STRANGE** sentence that you can have fun figuring out is "the rat the cat the dog chased killed ate the malt."

## 347 FAST FACT

📖 **THE WORD "UNDERGROUND"** is the only word that begins and ends with "und."

EGGCORN

Malapropism

BUSHISMS

MONDEGREENS     SPOONER

CUPERTINO                    MUPHRY'S, LAW

BAGSUND

TROUBLE

501

STRIFE

↓

# Common Howlers

PASTA BIBLE

TYPO

SPOONER

GREENGROCER'S

# EGGCORN

**SOUNDS LIKE A CUISINE,** doesn't it? It isn't. Eggcorn is the name given to a common howler that points to the mix-up between two similar sounding words. And guess what, even the origin of this term tells a story of a classic mix-up.

The story of how an "eggcorn" was born was first told by Chris Potts to Mark Liberman when he heard about a woman – let's call her Miss Take – who wrote down the word "eggcorn" while meaning an "acorn," a nut of the oak. Darling Miss Take barely knew that she had made a mistake.

When Mark Liberman heard about it, he couldn't help smiling and sharing this amusing tale on his website "Language Log" on September 23, 2003. When linguist Geoffrey Pullum stumbled upon this tid-bit he promptly opined that "eggcorn" should be apt to describe slip-ups such as these.

# MALAPROPISM

🎓 **THIS TERM IS USED TO DENOTE THE REPLACEMENT** of the correct word with the incorrect word, because they sound similar. Well, not as similar as eggcorns. Some of the incorrect replacements aren't even a real word in this case!

Where did the term Malapropism come from? The origin of this silly mistake can be traced back to the play "The Rivals: A Comedy" by Richard Brinsely Sheridan in 1775 that housed a character called Mrs Malaprop. The lady in question had the knack of using the most incorrect words ever. An example of her hilarious folly is: "He is the very pineapple of politeness." She meant pinnacle.

George W. Bush

But while Mrs Malaprop can be fondly remembered for giving birth to the term, there were others who have followed her example and amused us. George W. Bush stated: "We cannot let terrorists and rogue nations hold this nation hostile, or hold our allies hostile." He meant hostage.

## FAST FACT

📖 **GEORGE W. BUSH** was famous for his malapropisms. The term also came to be called as "Bushisms."

# MONDEGREENS

**WHILE ON THE TOPIC OF EVERYTHING** misheard and misrepresented, here's another term that's especially coined for misheard lyrics – Mondegreens. Do you relate to that one? Most of us do. Almost all of us have made up words for lyrics that we couldn't understand clearly. This happens because, while singing along with a song, we tend to fill up nebulous lyrics with similar sounding words.

And the story of Mondegreen – just like that of Malapropism and Eggcorns – tells the tale of a mistake. The woman who coined this term was author Sylvia Wright. It all happened when she was humming along with a Scottish ballad called "The Bonny Earl of Murray."

The ballad had the lyrics "Thou shall slay the Earl of Murray and laid him on the green," but do you know what Wright heard? She heard – "Thou shall slay the Earl of Murray and Lady Mondegreen." And that, friends, named a famous slip-up.

# REVEREND SPOONER AND HIS HILARIOUS SPOONERISMS

**SPOONERISMS POP UP WHEN LETTERS AND SOUNDS** get misplaced. Missed becomes hissed, flags becomes hags, so on and so forth. And while such errors do make us giggle, do you know why they are called Spoonerisms?

So here goes the story. There was a man called William Archibald Spooner who was born in London in 1844. He was associated with the Oxford University for 60 long years during which he lectured in history, philosophy, and divinity.

But he was albino, due to which his eyesight was poor, his face pink, and his body was too large for his head. Also, his speech always lagged behind his quick mind. This faulty make up gave rise to some of the most hilarious mix-ups in Spooner's life.

## FAST FACT

**THE MOST MEMORABLE ONE** was when Spooner was officiating a wedding, and he nudged the groom saying – "Son, it is now kisstomary to cuss the bride." There were many more, a long list that tumbled out of Spooner's fumbling mouth. And that's what led to such mix-ups being called as Spoonerisms.

# THE CUPERTINO EFFECT

**OKAY, SO THERE WAS A HOWLER – A MALAPROPISM,** a spoonerism, or a whatever there was in your copy that made your copy-editor bring out the nasty red pen. But what's this – the editor has replaced the errant word with a completely unfit one!

We sympathize with you. But, with a faint smile, we would also like to inform that the benevolent English language has a term for this issue too – "The Cupertino Effect."

The Cupertino effect was coined about a decade ago in 2000 by Elizabeth Muller. Muller had come across a case where an automated spell-checker was changing the unhyphenated word "cooperation" to "Cupertino," the name of a place in northern California. Muller wrote a piece about this issue in "Language Matters," a magazine by European Commission's English-language translators. And in her article named "Cupertino and After," Muller talked about a case in detail.

## FAST FACT

**MANY DOCUMENTS** from the United Nations, European Union, North Atlantic Treaty Organization, and other such international organizations were peppered with Cupertinos. That's what made this term popular and brought it to Muller's attention.

## 358 MURPHY'S LAW

 **ACCORDING TO** this funny editorial law, if you're pointing out errors in someone else's copy, especially in writing, your copy is bound to have errors too. Seems like such sweet revenge, doesn't it?

According to this law:

a. if you write anything criticizing while editing or proofreading, there will be a fault of some kind in what you have written;

b. if an author thanks you in a book for your editing or proofreading, there will be mistakes in the book;

c. the stronger the sentiment expressed in (a) and (b), the greater the fault;

d. any book devoted to editing or style will be internally inconsistent.

Courtesy: Language Log

## 359 FAST FACT

📖 **MURPHY'S LAW** came into existence in 1992. It was coined by John Bagsund in "The Society Of Editors" Newsletter.

## TROUBLE AND STRIFE IS A COCKNEY SLANG FOR WIFE

**NOW IF THAT ISN'T AMUSING,** what is? The Cockney Slang is a part of British English. The origin of this slang is a tad uncertain. There are some who believe that this kind of language came in handy for the thieves of London. But others are of the opinion that it was made popular by the lowly traders and shop keepers who needed to invent slangs that are unknown to customers to talk amongst themselves.

The lowly traders belonged to the worker's class of London. They were called Cockneys. That's how the term Cockney's slang came along. A characteristic of this slang is that it rhymes with the word it's referring to.

And so came by slangs like trouble and strife (wife), loaf of bread (one's head), pork pies (lies), and so on. While we know it's a tad difficult to get a hang of Cockney slang, using it in language gives an interesting edge to communication. You can even invent your own words too. Why, kids do it all the time at school. Even you must have done it.

## 361 HOW COSTLY CAN A HARMLESS TYPO GET?

**DO YOU KNOW WHAT THE WHOLE FUSS** over typos and silly mistakes is about? And why people are so particular about it? Because someone, in some part of the world, has paid heavily for their carelessness.

Take the case of the Bible published in 1631 by London's Baker Book house. The seventh directive listed in the 10 Commandments read: "Thou shalt commit adultery." Now that's a really grave mistake, isn't it? So the Parliament of that time ordered to destroy all the copies of this Bible, (it was named "The Wicked Bible") and made the London publisher pay a fine of 3000 pounds.

## 362 FAST FACT

**IN 2010, PENGUIN AUSTRALIA'S** "The Pasta Bible" instructed to season a dish with "salt and freshly ground black people!" Once the mistake came to light, the remaining 7,000 copies were destroyed on a sly; before anyone could take offense.

## WHY SOME GRAMMAR TEACHERS FREAK OUT AT THE SIGHT OF A SENTENCE BEGINNING WITH "AND."

**TO BEGIN A SENTENCE WITH "AND" IS** one of the most common howlers; don't you think? Here's a revelation – it's not so! It all happened in the beginning of 19th century when school teachers noticed that children loved to use the words "and" and "but." So much so, that they ended up using it every now and then. And it got a tad irritating.

These teachers decided to do something about it. However, instead of limiting the usage, they passed an order that "and" and "but" should not be used in the beginning of the sentence. It's a crime; a sin!

However, there isn't a single rule that will admonish the usage of these two connectives at the beginning of the sentence. Sorry, grammar teachers!

## FAST FACT

**"AND" HAS BEEN** spotted in oh-so-many texts written by Chaucer, Shakespeare, and Macaulay. Grammarian Henry Fowler referred to this mythical rule as a "superstition."

HERE IS
DARKNESS
BUT
IGNORANCE

## GREENGROCER'S APOSTROPHE

**A MISSED APOSTROPHE** or an apostrophe that's misplaced gives rise to many common howlers in English. While a missing apostrophe gives rise to unwanted plurals, an apostrophe when not needed is called a Greengrocer's Apostrophe.

This happens when you add 's instead of just s. The name of this howler stems from the fact that a grocer's list always misused the apostrophe and hence it came to be called as the Greengrocer's Apostrophe. For example, Pie's for $1 each.

SMS

160

CHARACTERS

TEXT SPEAK

JK

REBUS

LOL

BEG

ALOL

501

AWOL

# Grammar vs. the SMS Generation

OCSL

ROFLING

XOXO

VODAFONE

Lingo

# WHY IS A TEXT MESSAGE LIMITED TO 160 CHARACTERS?

**EVER WONDERED** why one text message amounts to 160 characters, and not 170 or 150? The story of this limit dates back to the mid 80s, when the committee organizing the telephone system was posed with the problem of setting a limit to the number of characters in a text message.

Friedhelm Hillebrand, who was a part of that committee, resolved the issue by typing out a sentence on his typewriter. He then counted the number of characters in that one sentence and decided that 160 characters should be enough for posing a question or answering it.

"This is perfectly sufficient," Hillebrand had said after the experiment in 1985, "perfectly sufficient." But the committee wasn't convinced. After all, there wasn't much research data to prove that 160 characters as a norm could be set for decades to follow. Would it be enough, they doubted?

So two arguments put forth and supported by Hillebrand were that, for one, postcards consisted less than 150 characters, and secondly, the telegraphy network for business professionals called "Telex" employed approximately the same number of characters.

So the character limit was set as 160. And we follow it till date!

## 367 FAST FACT...

📖 **JK IN TEXTSPEAK** refers to "just kidding."

## 368 FAST FACT...

📖 **IN 2007,** broadcaster John Humphrys criticized the use of SMS lingo in an article called "I h8 txt msgs: How texting is wreaking our language." The article was published in the "Daily Mail."

## FAST FACT...

📖 **WORDS AND SENTENCES** that are made by teaming up letters, numbers, or pictures are called Rebus. One example that we use in our day-to-day SMS lingo is "l8r," which is short for "later."

# LOL – LAUGH(ING) OUT LOUD ORIGINATED FROM LETTER WRITING

**HERE'S A REVELATION** – LOL's origin can't be confidently credited to the SMS lingo or Internet chat rooms. And that's because according to "The American Heritage Dictionary Of The English Language" LOL was initially used in letter-writing, and it stood for "Lots Of Luck" or "Lots Of Love."

What's more, LOL in Dutch isn't even an abbreviation, it's a word that's synonymous with fun. Then how, you may ask, did LOL manage to squeeze into our mobile phones or chat rooms?

Digging around reveals that LOL was probably used for the first time ever as an abbreviation for Laughing Out Loud (or something very similar) in a Bulletin Board System called "Viewline" in Canada when Wayne Pearson had LOLed on his friend's experience. "I found myself laughing out loud, echoing off the walls of my kitchen. That's when "LOL" was first used," he said in the 2008 list of popular internet initialisms from Computer World.

## FAST FACT...

**THE WORD** "BEG" in textspeak stands for "big evil grin."

## FAST FACT...

### 📖 WHAT'S ALOL?

This abbreviation stands for "Actually Laughing Out Loud." Did you know that?

## FAST FACT...

### 📖 AWOL

This lesser used term means "Absent Without Leave." Looks like SMS lingo has indeed broken into our formal spaces.

## FAST FACT...

### 📖 WHAT'S OCSL?

A brand new slang that's just made its entry into the world of abbreviations is OCSL – "On the Chair Stifling Laughter," for all those who can't picture themselves ROFLing (Rolling on the floor laughing). Interesting?

## WHY XOXO STANDS FOR HUGS AND KISSES

🎓 **YOU MUST HAVE** seen these four caps-locked letters at the end of mails or text messages. And you know they mean "hugs and kisses." Awwwie! But have you ever wondered why they mean so? It's definitely not an acronym by any angle. So what is it?

Careful research reveals that in the Middle Ages, when people weren't aware of proper letters or styles of signature, they signed at the end of the document with an X and kissed it in the name of Christ, to show that they plan to keep the promise, or in honor of the agreement.

But that was for the Christians. Jewish immigrants, who also had difficulty in signing the agreements, signed with an O that some historians believe refer to a solemn, respectful hug. The Jewish immigrants couldn't use X because their beliefs were different from that of the Christians.

Gradually, these symbols of hugs and kisses came together to form XOXO. But the facts about when this symbol was first used are still hazy.

## FAST FACT...

📖 The **FIRST SMS SENT WAS "MERRY CHRISTMAS."**
It happened in 1992 when engineer Neil Papworth sent the first ever SMS to Vodafone executive Richard Jarvis.

Merry Christmas

## 377 FAST FACT...

📖 **WHAT DOES** SMS stand for? It's an abbreviation for "Short Messaging Service."

## 378 FAST FACT...

📖 **GET DIVORCED VIA SMS!** It might sound shocking, even rude, but it's true. The Islamic Sharia law acknowledges that a divorce can happen over an SMS that's clear and unambiguous.

## 379 FAST FACT...

📖 **BABIES TO BE NAMED IN SMS LANGUAGE** While purists were busy fretting over keeping SMS lingo away from lengthy texts, parents who are gung-ho about this culture have decided to follow the SMS culture while naming their babies too! For example, Cameron has been cut short to Cam'ron. And that's just the beginning, folks!

twitter.com

...w Twitter experience is coming! Learn more about it... #

# THE DICTIONARY IS OPENING UP TO SMS LINGO

**LOLz! TAKE THAT, YOU NAYSAYERS**. The Oxford English Dictionary Online is opening up to rapidly changing vocabulary and trying to accommodate words like LOLz and mwahahaha in its crammed self. And a glance at their meaning reveals that LOLz stands for fun, laughter, or amusement, while mwahahaha is an evil, villainous laugh!

What's more, short-forms continue to be a rage, and the dictionary has also made way for the short form of ridiculous – ridic. And while on this topic of new-age words, how can we forget the influential Twitter? Going by its popularity, OED has also included the Twitter term "tweeps" in its vocabulary. Tweeps stands for "followers" on Twitter.

Will school teachers still object to the use of such words in the exam papers? Time to raise a doubt, students.

## FAST FACT...

**DON'T SHOUT!** Typing in all caps is considered as shouting in SMS lingo.

## 382 FAST FACT...

📖 **THE LANGUAGE** of SMS is known as Textspeak.

## 383 FAST FACT...

📖 **"I THINK WE'RE LIVING** in a time when our ears are attuned to a flattened and truncated sense of our English language, so this always begs the question, is Shakespeare relevant?" – Actor Ralph Fiennes commented on changing form of language on Twitter.

## 384 FAST FACT...

📖 **MRS IS NOT THE SHORT FORM** of Misus; it's short for mistress. Unlike now, mistress in the olden days didn't hold a negative connotation. She was just the "she-master" of the house.

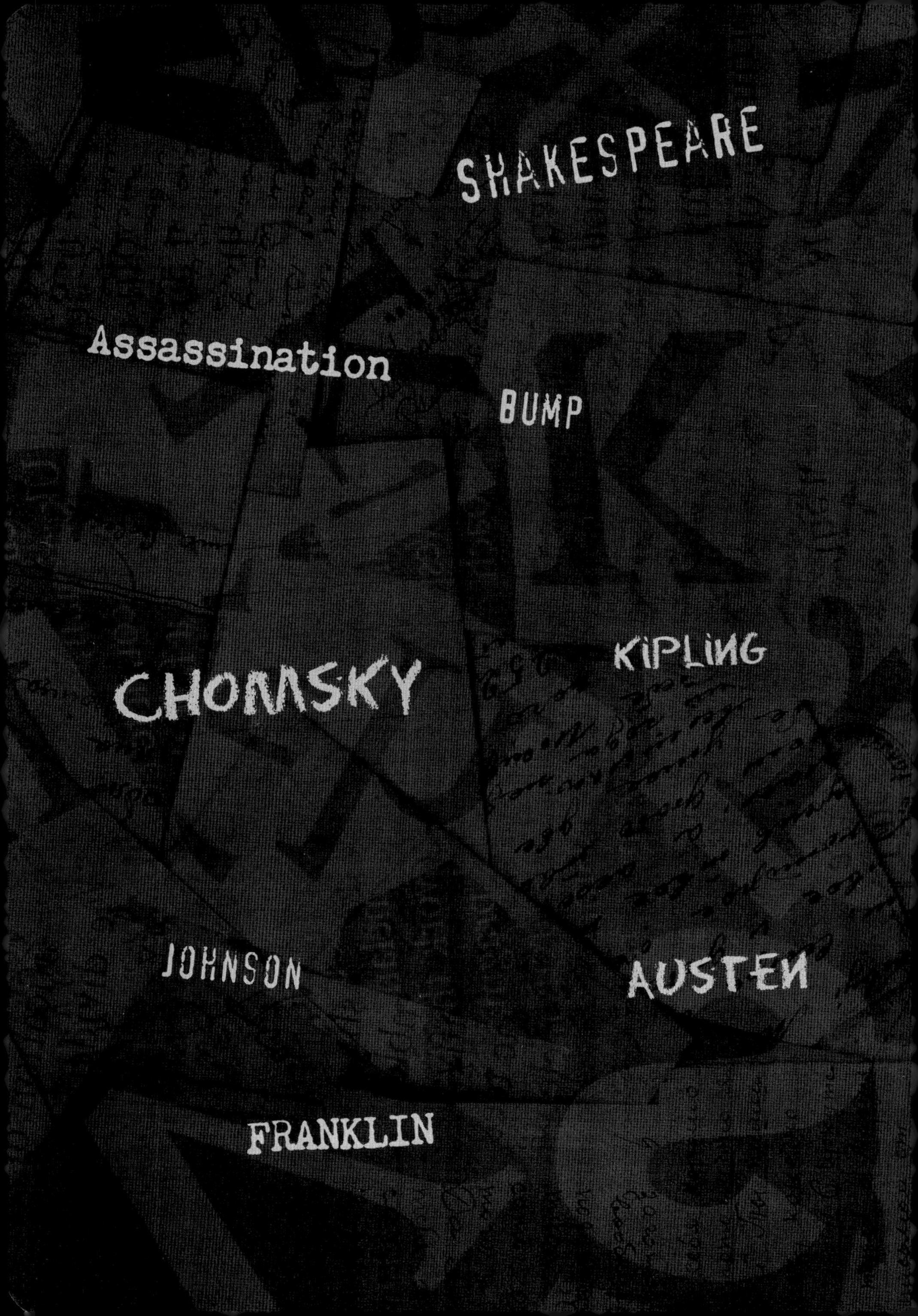

SHAKESPEARE

Assassination

BUMP

KIPLING

CHOMSKY

JOHNSON

AUSTEN

FRANKLIN

DICKENS

501

WEBSTER

↓

# Grammar and
# the Stalwarts ←

SPELLINGS

SILENT

JOHNSON

DICTIONARY

KIPLING

# SHAKESPEARE LOVED SWITCHING THE FUNCTION OF A WORD

**WILLIAM SHAKESPEARE** has intelligently fiddled with the English language. We know, you know. But he had one characteristic that blew people away, literally. And that was to switch the function of a word.

Switching the function of a word refers to the practice of converting a verb into a noun, or an adjective into a verb. This kind of conversion is known as a functional switch. And Shakespeare, who wasn't a huge fan of the rigid grammar rules, loved playing around with words and changing their functions. For e.g., in "He words me" the genius playwright uses" words," a common noun, as a verb.

## FAST FACT...

**SHAKESPEARE WAS** an actor. He played the role of the ghost in "Hamlet" and of Adam in "As you like it." But he was so busy writing and making plays that he could only take up tiny roles in them.

THERE IS NO DARKNESS BUT IGNORANCE

## 387 GRAMMAR WASN'T WILLIAM SHAKESPEARE'S FORTE

**WILLIAM SHAKESPEARE** might have been a genius when it came to story-telling or vocabulary. He had almost double the number of words crammed in his vocab than a layman. But when it came to grammar, Shakespeare's track record isn't a shiny one. The stalwart faltered in this field.

But Shakespeare could be forgiven for not following the rules of Grammar in those times. Why? Because the rules we follow oh-so-solemnly these days hardly existed! Yes, grammar stalwarts were absent in Shakespearean times, and so were Grammar teachers. Writers were mostly on their own, devising their own rules.

It was almost 150 years after William Shakespeare's death that the Grammar teachers started tightening their hold. The decay of English after the death of Elizabeth Age was what gave rise to this sudden stir-up. English men feared that if the language doesn't get bound in a set of rules, it might lose its essence.

## FAST FACT...

 **THE EPITAPH** on Shakespeare's grave read: "Curst be he that moves my bones."

## FAST FACT...

**SHAKESPEARE INVENTED** the words "assassination" and "bump."

198

# NOAM CHOMSKY BELIEVES GRAMMAR IS INSTINCTIVE

**ACCORDING TO** Noam Chomsky, who is a thinker, grammar is of a universal kind. It is embedded deep into the conscience of human beings. Chomsky states that certain basic rules of grammar can't be taught; they are not, in fact. Yet, a little child, who struggles to expand his measly vocabulary, gets a knack of how the words are to be strung together for them to sound right. And it is this knack that Chomsky stresses upon.

Noam Chomsky

Chomsky calls them super-rules, and believes that they are embedded in the genetic structure. A child who is growing amidst people speaking a particular kind of language grasps certain rules of its syntax that aren't taught. A sentence is formed in a particular way in every language. And the child, on listening to such constructions, gets the hang of it.

A classic example that's put forth by the great thinker in his book "Syntactic Structures" that deals with syntax and how certain sentences just sound right without a tangible reason, is: Colorless green ideas sleep furiously. This sentence seems to be more right than: Furiously sleep ideas green colorless.

## FAST FACT...

📖 **RUDYARD KIPLING** faced a nasty rejection in 1889 when the editor of the San Francisco Examiner informed him, "I'm sorry Mr Kipling, but you just don't know how to use the English language."

Rudyard Kipling

### FAST FACT...

📖 **SAMUEL JOHNSON** barely made any money, even after "The Dictionary Of English Language" was published on April 15, 1755. His status was lifted only after he was awarded the government pension in 1762.

### FAST FACT...

📖 **FIVE EDITIONS** of "The Dictionary of English Language" were published when Samuel Johnson was alive.

### FAST FACT...

📖 **SAMUEL JOHNSON** took approximately nine years to compile "The Dictionary of English Language."

# JANE AUSTEN WASN'T PERFECT WITH HER GRAMMAR AND SPELLINGS

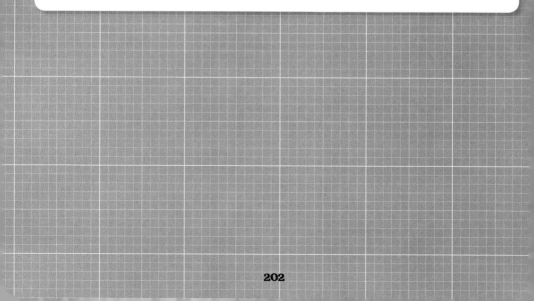

**WHILE WE FONDLY** remember Jane Austen as the author of the classics "Pride and Prejudice," "Sense and Sensibility," and "Emma" amongst the others, it's no longer a secret that Austen's grammar and spelling was a tad messy.

Professor Kathryn Sutherland, who studied 1,100 pages handwritten by Jane revealed in an interview, "She (Jane Austen) broke most of the rules of writing good English."

What's more, letters that went to-and-fro between Jane and her publisher John Murray II reveal that the finished novel had a strong presence of Murray's favorite editor William Gifford, who was entrusted with the task of cleaning up Jane's language.

Wouldn't you love to get a copy of the books before Gifford set to work on them?

## 396 FAST FACT...

📖 **"GREAT BOOKS** are weighed and measured by their style and matter, and not the trimmings and shadings of their grammar." – Mark Twain.

## 397 FAST FACT...

📖 **BUFFON HAS** an old saying - "The man himself is as near the truth as we can get - but then most men mistake grammar for style, as they mistake correct spelling for words or schooling for education."
Samuel Butler

## FAST FACT...

📖 **BENJAMIN FRANKLIN** tried to reform English language by suggesting that the letters c, j, q, w, x, and y should be replaced by two new vowels and four new consonants.

Benjamin Franklin

Charles Dickens

## FAST FACT...

📖 **"DO YOU SPELL** it with a "V" or a "W"?" inquired the judge. "That depends upon the taste and the fancy of the speller, my Lord," replied Sam. - Charles Dickens, The Pickwick Papers.

## 400 NOAH WEBSTER WANTED TO DO AWAY WITH THE SILENT LETTERS

**NOAH WEBSTER,** who is remembered for the making of the "American Dictionary of English Language" (1828) was influenced by George Bernard Shaw's ideas. So, 40 years before he published the American dictionary, he proposed loads of changes in the way we spell words.

For example, he wanted to omit all the silent letters thereby turning "bread" into "bred," and "friend" into "frend." He also wanted to do away with the confusing "ea" or "ie." "Mean," in that case would have become "meen."

But very few of his suggestions actually made it to the final American Dictionary Of English Language.

# NOAH WEBSTER PUBLISHED HIS OWN VERSION OF BIBLE

**NOAH WEBSTER,** who was first busy protesting against defunct letters in English, later turned his attention to King James's Bible. Webster considered this Bible to be full of grammatical errors and lewd words. So he took it upon himself to make the holy book look more presentable. "I consider this emendation of the common version as the most important enterprise of my life," Webster had confessed.

Most of the grammatical errors disappeared from the text. So did other words like fornication, spew, and slay which were replaced with lewdness, vomit, and kill.

Noah Webster's bible was published in 1833.

## FAST FACT...

📖 **THE BLUE-BACK** speller
is the dictionary created by
Noah Webster that houses the
American spellings.

MERRY

Salt

SALARY

DAVID CRYSTAL

SIMPSONS

BRAT

FUNGIBLE

FUNGUS  ARSY

501

GUY

# Linguists-Study of Language and Grammar

BOOZE

WEDNESDAY

RECIPE

FOPDOODLE

GLAMOUR

## WHERE DID THE "MERRY" COME FROM IN MERRY CHRISTMAS?

**"MERRY" IS A VERY OLD WORD.** Really old. But it didn't look as merry as it does now. The word first made an appearance in the 9th century in an old manuscript written by King Alfred. And it was spelt "myrige." The "y" was to be pronounced like the "i" in fit, albeit with rounded lips.

But the fashion of rounding one's lips passed. And by the Middle Ages, "myrige" changed to "mirye." However the spelling remained unstable, changing at every turn.

It was by the 14th century that "merry" came to be spelled like we do it today. Merry, as we know it now, stood for "something that causes pleasure." And so, somewhere in the 1780, merry-bout came to be used as a low slang that referred to "an incident of sexual intercourse."

## FAST FACT

**A RECORD** exists in the 1565 in "The Hereford Municipal Manuscript" that said: "And thus I comytt you to god, who send you a mery Christmas and many."

## DO YOU WANT SALT AS SALARY?

**A ROMAN SOLDIER 2000 YEARS** ago would have happily nodded in affirmation. And that's what brings us to the story of how the word "salary" developed.

In the middle of the 14th century, salt was handed to the workers, Roman soldiers actually, as their daily wages. Back then, as soldiers went to war and had to stay away from home for long periods of time, they used salt to preserve their food. They did some sort of pickling, perhaps. And for that it was necessary to procure salt. Or their food would rot and they would die.

What's more, salt was a highly priced possession back then and was used as a part of Egyptian religious offerings. So in those days, when someone said "your salt's worth" they literally meant it. And slowly, the mode of payment came to be termed as "salary."

## FAST FACT

**ENGLISH WAS** called the thief of languages because it borrowed words (shamelessly?) from other languages. David Crystal called it the vacuum cleaner of languages in his book "The Story of English in 100 Words." Words from the neighboring languages would get sucked in, Crystal reported.

# 407 THANK THE SIMPSONS FOR "MEH"

🎓 **THE WORD "MEH" REFERS TO BOREDOM OR INDIFFERENCE.** And it tip-toed into our English vocabulary in the early 2000s when "The Simpsons," an American adult animated sitcom, began using it sporadically.

The conversation between Homer, Lisa, and Bart that first brought "meh" to the limelight was:

Homer: Kids, how would you like to go to Blocko Island?

Lisa and Bart: Meh.

Homer: But the TV gave me the impression that...

Bart: We said "meh."

Lisa. M-E-H. Meh.

A piece in the Boston Globe suggests that "meh" has Yiddish origins, and that the word wasn't a new one in Yiddish. It was a part of the Yiddish-English dictionary of 1928 and "meh" was defined as an interjection and adjective meaning "be as it may" or "so-so."

In 2008, the Collins English Dictionary defined "meh" with "an interjection to suggest indifference or boredom" or as an adjective to say something is mediocre or a person is unimpressed.

Some even believed that "eeh" by a chance mistake gave rise to "meh." But that's not so.

# WHERE DID THAT WORD "BRAT" COME FROM?

**BRAT, A WORD THAT REFERS TO** an ill-behaved children, has its origins in Britain during the 1500s. In those days, brat stood for a beggar's child. And mind you, we aren't referring to the children hiding behind the ragged counters of their parents.

In those times, pretty much like today, a beggar's children were out on display. People with change clinking in their pockets could sympathize and offer some coins to the poor. Not to forget, the behavior of most of the beggar children wasn't really impeccable, either. If nostalgic reports are to be believed, they annoyed the passers-by, and how!

And that's why, when Samuel Johnson compiled the "Dictionary of English Language" in 1755, he defined brat as "a child, so called in contempt."

So that's where the word "brat" comes from. But the brat of today isn't a child in rags, but one who belongs to the upper strata of the society.

## FAST FACT

**TO CANCEL AN** inauguration is to "exaugurate." Yes, there is a word like that!

## FAST FACT

**"KUDOS" HAS BEEN** around in the form of "kudo" since 1926. It's a word of Greek origin, which means "glory" or "fame."

## 411 IS FUNGIBLE RELATED TO FUNGUS?

**SOMETIMES, WE ASSUME** the meanings of words based on their sounds. They sound like something we may have heard before. One such word is fungible, which looks like it's closely related to fungus.

Here's the catch. It's not so. It's a legal term that represents goods or money that can be replaced with items worth the equivalent. It comes from the Latin word "fungi vice" which means "to take place."

## 412 FAST FACT

**IN 1950s** only the upper-classes of Britain had lunch. Everyone else had dinner. So lunch and dinner had nothing to do with the time of the day.

## 413 FAST FACT

**ARSY IN BRITAIN** means arrogant, but in Australia it means lucky.

## WHY IS IT A WEDNESDAY?

**LIKE EACH DAY OF THE WEEK IS DEDICATED** to one God, even Wednesday gets its name from the Anglo-Saxon God "Woden," also known commonly as Mercury. This particular God had been thrust with the responsibilities of curing horses, carrying messages, and carrying the dead.

So in those sepia-tinged times, Wednesday evolved through names like Wodnesdaeg, Weodnesdei, Wenysday, Wonysday, and Weddinsday. Why, even William Shakespeare coined his own version of the name as Wensday. Finally, what we got on our plates and in our bulky dictionaries was "Wednesday."

This day in the middle of the week is also known as a Hump day, because it comes bang in the middle. Usually by this day you know where your week is headed and it holds the maximum possibilities of promises and hopes. If you draw a graph of the days of the week, this day is what will make a peak, or a hump.

### FAST FACT

**THE WORD "DUDE" POPPED** in English in 1883, New York. Since then, its popularity has spread far and wide. However, the person or the reason behind the coinage of this term remains anonymous.

### FAST FACT

**TO FART** silently is to "fist."

## 417 WHY BOOZE?

**THE WORD BOOZE IS USED OH-SO-COMMONLY.** It's more common than "drinks" or "alcohol," at least among younger people. But what could be said about its origin?

Many believe that the word comes from the name of a popular distiller. But no, it wasn't a term coined by a distiller in the US named EC Booze in the 19th century, although many would like to believe so. EC Booze just happens to be a real life aptronym.

So where did booze come from? A hard look at its journey will reveal that its origins lies in the dutch word "busen." It meant "to drink excessively." When this drunken word staggered into the English vocabulary in the 14th century it became "bouse."

"Booze," the word that we use today, came into usage in the 17th century.

## 418 FAST FACT

**GLAMOUR SURPRISINGLY** stems from the word "grammar." When "grammarye" – a word that stood for occult learning – came to be used by people from the occult realm, its pronunciation was changed to "glamor," which they used to cast a glamor.

## 419 FAST FACT

**SAUSAGE DOESN'T** originate from the word sauce. It comes from the Greek word "salsus," meaning salted meat. Greeks in ancient times salted their meat to preserve it.

## RX STANDS FOR RECIPE

**SEEING THIS ACRONYM** on a prescription might have led you to believe that it stands for something very complicated. After all it refers to the bombastic names of scary medicines.

But it isn't so. Rx means recipe. In Latin that refers to "to take." And doctors used to write down the recipe for getting well – the medicines. But there's more to it. The X part of the symbol represents a prayer to the Roman God Jupiter to make the cure work. And this stems from the Roman belief that we fall ill when we offend the Gods.

So that was why Rx has traveled on our prescriptions since the Roman era. But while the Rx of the olden days said prayers and instructed us to take medicines, the Rx of today insists that the drug to be bought should be prescribed by a certified physician only.

### FAST FACT

**PANTS, OR THE** short form of pantaloons was considered to be a dirty, vulgur word.

### FAST FACT

**THE WORD THAT** denotes day before yesterday is "nudiustertian." And it is derived from the Latin word "nudius tertius" meaning "relating to the day before yesterday."

## 423    A FOPDOODLE IS DOUBLE THE FOOL

**BUT YOU WOULDN'T HAVE COME** to know about it had you not stumbled across this fact. Because the word no longer exists in the dictionary you refer to.

The word was used in the 17th century and is a mash-up of the words "fop" (a fool) and "doodle" (a simpleton). But as time went by, the Editors whose opinions really mattered and who decided what does or doesn't go into a dictionary opined that fopdoodle is barely being looked up. "What a waste of space!" they must've exclaimed. And it was promptly chucked out.

Other words that were shown the door were "smellfeast" (a parasite) and "grody" (dirty, nasty).

## 424    FAST FACT

**ONE "MOMENT" COMPRISES** of 90 seconds. This fact was first documented by Cornish writer John of Trevisa who wrote that 40 moments make an hour. The Oxford English Dictionary later described a moment as "a very brief period of time."

## 425    FAST FACT

**"WIDDIFUL" IS** a person who deserves to be hanged.

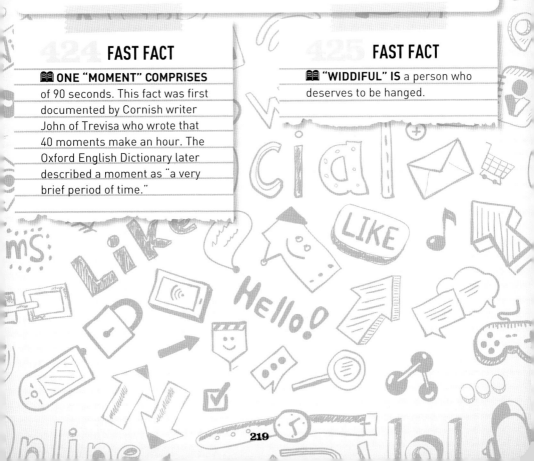

## DOES THE WORD "GUY" REFER TO A GROTESQUE LOOKING PERSON?

**THE WORD "GUY"** comes from the name Guido (Guy) Fawkes, who was responsible for conspiring a blast in the English House of Parliament on November 5, 1605. He had concealed 36 barrels of gun-powder to blow up King James I and the Parliament. Fortunately, his plan failed. He was caught and executed.

Post that, November 5 came to be called as Guy Fawkes Day, which was considered to be similar to American Halloween. Boys dressed grotesquely stepped out of the house to collect treats.

And that's how the word "guy" entered the English vocabulary.

## FAST FACT

**CHECKMATE ORIGINATES** from the Persian term "Shah mat." Checkmate in chess means that the king is left helpless, and is one step away from being stumped. So "Shah" in Persian means "king" and "mat" indicates that he is dead.

## FAST FACT

**THE WORD "GRAMMAR"** originated from the Greek word "grammatike techne" which represents the "art of letters."

## 429 BRUNCH IS A PORTMANTEAU

🎓 **PORTMANTEAU IS A WORD** formed by joining halves of two words. For e.g., "brunch" is made from the words "breakfast" and "lunch." But whoever coined such a term for these amalgamations?

The story of portmanteau dates back to the 1580s, when portmanteau only stood for traveling bag. It's a French word. And it would've remained just that. But Lewis Carroll used the word slithy (slimy and lithe) to describe Jabberwocky, the monster, in 1882. And that was when he used portmanteau to refer to his invention – two words packaged into one.

Today we see names of celebs fusing into one another, forming some famous portmanteaus, like Brangelina.

## 430 FAST FACT

📖 **FLOCCINAVICINIHILIPILIFICATION** is one of the longest words in the English language, and it originates from the culmination of native words flocci, nauci, nihili, and pili. All these words refer to little or no value.

## 431 FAST FACT

📖 **"SHITFACED" MEANT "YOUNG-LOOKING"** in the Scottish dictionary. Yes, prior to 1826, shitfaced, according to Scottish dictionary meant small-faced. It referred to someone who had boyish or young looks.

## MUGGLE – NON-MAGICAL, A DRUG-DEALER, A SWEETHEART OR A FISH–LIKE TAIL?

**HARRY POTTER FANS MIGHT VOUCH FOR "A FOOL."** That's because JK Rowling used the word "muggle "to describe a non-magical person in her first Harry Potter novel in 1997. But soon after that, in 2000, muggle was used as a slang to refer to marijuana, and the person who dealt with it was a muggler. But JK Rowling's muggle wins the popularity contest. Muggle as marijuana is prevalent only in the dark alleys of drug-dealers in America, perhaps.

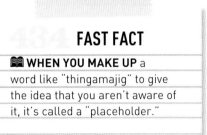

Even so, those aren't the only meanings that have tagged along with the word. In the 13th century, muggle represented a fish-like tail and in the 17th century, it stood for sweetheart.

So what meaning do you want to go with?

## FAST FACT

**THE WORD HYSTERIA** originates from the Greek term "hystera" which means ovary or womb. It got coined in the Victorian era when the vagina of an hysterical female would be shot with a strong stream of water to calm her down.

## FAST FACT

**WHEN YOU MAKE UP** a word like "thingamajig" to give the idea that you aren't aware of it, it's called a "placeholder."

# SINCE WHEN DID "BLOODY" BECOME A SWEAR WORD?

**"BLOODY" LITERALLY MEANT BLOOD-STAINED** when used by the Anglo-Saxons. But in 1711, Jonathan Swift wrote a letter to Stella that described hot as "bloody hot" meaning "very hot." The meaning of this word was slowly but steadily shifting base.

## FAST FACT

**JUST LIKE SAUSAGE,** the Greek word for salted vegetables was coined as salad.

The word was all fine till the 18<sup>th</sup> century, when certain aristocrats, whose minds conjured up blood-stained and gory images at the mention of the word bloody, protested against the use of this graphic word amongst the respectable people.

The word bloody was described as "very vulgar" by Dr Johnson in his dictionary.

## 437 JAZZ WAS CHOSEN AS THE WORD OF THE CENTURY BY THE AMERICAN DIALECT SOCIETY

**IN 2010, WHEN THE WORD "GOOGLE" WAS** chosen to be the word of the year, "jazz" was chosen to be the word of the century. The word's been around for, well, almost a century. And it did signify a perceptible shift in the culture of music, right? So we can't really grudge jazz its success.

But here's something about the word of the century that very few people know. Jazz didn't begin its career as a musical genre. Jazz, when it was born around 1913, stood for excitement. "All that jazz," an expression we use even now referred to things like that. The word slowly came to have sauve, sophisticated connotations.

It was first used to describe music in 1915, a moment recorded by the Chicago press. It was an instant hit, and it kind of named an era.

In 1950s, we had jazzercise – exercising to jazz beats and jazzetry – reading poetry to jazz. We also had jazz cigarettes, a term that referred to marijuana, in the 1990s.

Does this fact make you look at "jazz" with a newfound respect?

# WHAT'S REALLY OK?

**IF SOMEONE WHO REALLY WANTS TO KNOW** about the etymology of OK will face numerous confusing alleys. English has picked its fragments from oh-so-many languages. In which direction do we look while tracing the origin of OK?

Does it originate from the French "au quai," Scottish "och aye," Choctaw "oke," Wolof "okeh" or Latin "omnis korrecta"? Before your head begins to spin, know that it's from none of these.

Thanks to American lexicographer Allan Walker Read we know that OK originated from an unassuming language game in the Boston newspaper in 1839.
OK in that game stood for Oll Korrect. It was just a game, and there was no such real word. So why did OK stick around while we have no clue about the other abbreviations that got formed?

In 1840, OK left oll korrect's residence and housed itself in President Martin Van Buren–Kinderhook's short-form Old Kinderhook. OK became popular during the elections of 1840, thanks to all the canvassing.

Martin Van Buren

There was also a Democratic OK club, members of which were called OK.

Such changes, and that too in a short period of time, led to some hotch-potch. Emerging from all the confusion was an OK that meant – all right, good.

All's well that ends well, isn't it?

Charles Dickens

## 439 AIN'T GOOD?

**WHILE WORDS LIKE CAN'T, DON'T, AND SHAN'T** were added to the English vocabulary in the 1600s, "ain't" arrived a tad later. It first made its appearance as an't. Its use is documented in "Love for Love," a play by William Congreve in 1695. "You need not sit so near one, if you have anything to say. I can hear you farther off, I an't deaf."

Such abbreviated forms were welcomed by writers like Jonathan Swift who wrote in Journal of Stella in 1710 – "An't you an impudent slut?" And that brings us to the question that if "an't" was such a popular and much-talked-about word, how did an "i" figure in it?

In the olden times, the letter "a" in an't was pronounced as "ay." So gradually it gave rise to the usage of "i" in the spelling to make it sound phonetically correct. This happened some time in the 18th century.

"Ain't" sort of became a favorite of authors and it got picked up in colloquial American English. Although authors like Charles Dickens used it to show the dialect of the upper middle class.

## SOCIALISE OVER TEA

**WE HAVE SOCIAL NETWORKING SITES TODAY,** but in the ancient times we had "tea." A peek into the diary of Samuel Pepys reveals that tea was spelled as tee – "I did send for a cup of tee (a China drink) of which I never had drunk before," he wrote on September 25, 1660.

The drink was first introduced to Queen Catherine, the Portuguese wife of King Charles II in 1661. It was an instant hit.

"Tea-time" began to be a time for people to socialize and gossip. Slowly, "tea" spread its wings, rather leaves, over various words that revolved around a tea-drinking session, such as the tea-cup, tea-pot, tea-spoon, even tea-dish, and tea-room.

"Tea" in British English came to be regarded as the drink itself, along with some light refreshments like scones and sandwiches. What if all you want to enjoy is just a cup of tea? In that case, it is called a "spot of tea." A phrase coined by the Americans.

The tea world is still spreading and the latest one that hopped in is "tea-brained," an obtuse person.

King Charles II

## ROYAL OR REGAL?

**IF THE SHRUG SUGGESTING – WHAT DIFFERENCE DOES IT MAKE?** – is on the way, then stop it right there! There is a difference. If you take a look at the history of these terms, you will know.

First of all, the words "regal" and "royal" weren't even a part of the Anglo-Saxon vocabulary. There was king/queen-like or kingly and queenly.

What if you don't just want to refer to the grandeur of the king or queen? What if you want to talk about the lavishness or the power of the entire kingly/queenly family? It gets a little complicated, doesn't it? After a lot of deliberation, "royal" and "regal" got picked.

The connotations of royal related to heritage, whereas connotations of regal pointed to power and rule. Regal originates from the Latin word "regis," meaning the king. Royal has its roots in the French word "roial" which means on a grand scale.

## 442 FAST FACT

**THE NAME "ENGLISH"** made an appearance first. From that originated the name "England."

Queen Sylvia and King Harald of Sweden

French President Nocholas Sarkozt with Spanish King Juan Carlos I

# WHERE DID ENGLISH COME FROM?

**WE'VE TALKED** a lot about English, but what about the origin of the word that refers to this language? English, many believed, is derived from the word England. But it's not so. It's actually vice versa. How did the word "English" come around?

We know that the language primarily refers to the tongue of the Anglo-Saxons. Back then, the three most important nations of Germany set foot on British Isles. They were the Angles, Saxons, and Jutes. Two of them gave rise to a powerful community – the Anglo-Saxons.

But in the 8th century, Latin writers pointed at the Anglo Saxons as Angli Saxons. This was pivotal in the naming of English as the Anglo Saxons later came to be called as the English Saxons.

The name of the language of Anglo-Saxons came to be "Englisc," and then "English."

## 444 FAST FACT...

**THE PRONUNCIATION** of En- gradually changed to In- but the spelling remained English.

## 445 ARE Y'ALL ENJOYING?

🎓 **WE KNOW THAT** the apostrophe fills in for missing letters. But who stumbled this way first? How did "you all" come to be shortened to "y'all?" Sit tight, because here's the story.

At the beginning of the 19th century, people pondered over how to address a group of people as "you." They invented words like yees, yiz, yez, or yeez whenever the speaker talked to more than one person. But nothing got standardized.

There was also the classic case of adding an "s" to plural, and some Irishmen resorted to talk to "yous." But gradually even the "s" faded away and we were back to the problem. Thou had gone out of fashion, so the use wasn't encouraged, except if you were rehearsing for a Shakespearean play.

Somewhere in the early 19th century in the southern states of USA, where the use of words differed quite a bit, a wise man came up with the phrase "you all." Initially, it was plural, but it came to be used for addressing a singular person too. That was the basic difference in usage.

Soon, "y'all" was in. The way people use it in different states of course differed. But the word was in!

## 446 FAST FACT...

📖 **EDITRESS** is a word for the female editor. Yes, it is! It became quite popular in the 19th century, but soon went out of fashion.

## A GAZETTE IS NOT A NEWSPAPER

**GAZETTE, GAZETTA,** and gazeta are French, Italian, and Venetian words for a newspaper. When the word was first borrowed by the English language, it stood for newspaper. A note of thanks should be given to the Oxford Gazette, the first newspaper to be published in 1665. Here's a story about how Oxford Gazette came around.

It was a time in history when King Charles II had to shift office due to the Great Plague and relocate to London. To keep him updated with the daily going-ons of the city, publisher Henry Muddiman was entrusted with the duty of publishing the gazette. Later, it went on to become the London Gazette.

But a gazette was an uptight formal copy. Frivolous gossip didn't look good in it. So a newspaper was born to house the light, fluffy talks. Gazettes existed, but as formal journals.

Got the difference?

## FAST FACT...

**RUDYARD KIPLING** coined the word "curtiosity," which was a stunt-word, a word that the author uses as a chance, or a stunt. If it grabs attention, well and good. If not, it's lost once the book is slapped shut. Another such word is "misunderestimate."

Rudyard Kipling

# 449 WHY DID THE "E" DISAPPEAR FROM POTATO?

**THE POTATOE** had an "e" in the earlier times. People weren't comfortable using a word ending with –o. That was the characteristic of Italian imports such as portico, volcano, etc. So an –e was added.

For more than one potatoe, just add an s and you have a plural that we use till date. But there was also the Green Grocer's Apostrophe that was a rage in those times. Many even resorted to calling plural potatoes as potato's.

The spelling that finally got standardized for the plural was potatoes, and the "e" was chucked from the singular, thanks to Dan Quayle, vice-president of USA, 1992, who misspelled while officiating at a spelling bee. Even then, the spelling "potatoe" lingered around to create problems in spelling bee contests.

Quayle's case brought this confusion to limelight. After that, the "e" promptly got dropped. Sadly, Quayle earned quite the bad reputation for it.

## FAST FACT...

**JOHNSON ACTUALLY** stood for son of John. Similar is the story of other names that end with "son."

## FAST FACT...

**POTATO WAS** used to refer to money, as in "have you got the potato worth to buy it?" as slang in America.

233

# STREETS WEREN'T ALWAYS IN OUR NEIGHBORHOOD

**THE ENGLISH WORD** street has been derived from the Latin word "strata" or "stratum," which meant divisions. The Romans used this word to refer to the straight, long roads that they had built.

Those long roads weren't the only places where this word was used. Street gave birth to the phrase "by the sty," which means "by the street," and came to be referred to as a "happening in the public," or something that's "happening everywhere."

Similarly, another phrase that was erected by the support of this word was "on the street," which meant prostitution. But "people on the street" meant the common man. "Man on the street" in 1831 became an ordinary person, and "street people," a term that emerged in 1967, referred to those who lived on the streets, or the homeless.

# 453   SILLY WASN'T FOOLISH WHEN IT BEGAN ITS JOURNEY

**"SILLY" WAS** the child of the Old English word "seely," which meant happy or blessed in the 11th century. It was derived from the German word "selig," which meant "blessed." Look at what it means now! Shocking, isn't it? That's how the norm's been for the English language.

The word "seely" was happily housed in the dictionary. But an ignorant chap mistook its plain happiness for a child's naïve happiness. That led to a slight tweak in its meaning.

After that, silly's meanings kept changing from innocent, harmless, pitiable, feeble, and finally to stupid, or foolish. Now, we have a silly word that tells the story of a silly mistake.

This kind of practice is called "pejoration," which is reducing the worth of a word. Just like silly went from being happy to downright foolish.

## 454   FAST FACT...

📖 **THE TERM "JABBERWOCKY"** represents made-up nonsense. It came around when Lewis Carroll wrote a poem that made least sense in 1871 and called it Jabberwocky in the book "Looking Through The Glass, and What Alice Found There."

## 455   FAST FACT...

📖 **"HOOLIGAN"** originated from the word "hoolihan," which referred to an Irish man involved in a bar fight. Does that make it a racist term?

# WHAT DOES QWERTY MEAN?

**WE'VE USED** the term time and again, especially in a mobile shop. QWERTY is a kind of keypad. Have you ever wondered who coined such a bizarre name? A revelation is that the term wasn't coined after swanky new phones with such keypads that flooded the market. The QWERTY keypad has been around for years, on typewriters. The first six letters on the keyboard of a typewriter or a computer are Q,W,E,R,T, and Y. Such a keyboard is called a "universal" keyboard. It was invented by CL Sholes.

When the same arrangement of letters began to be followed on new-age mobile keypads, QWERTY became a rage.

## FAST FACT...

**IN MEDIEVAL EUROPE,** women were considered to be adjective creatures as the term "adjective" means "unable to stand alone."

## FAST FACT...

**BEFORE BECOMING** synonymous to homosexuals, the term "queer" stood "eccentric'" in Scottish, and "odd" and "perverse" in German. It was only in 1922 that "queer" began to stand for homosexuals.

## FAST FACT...

**SNARL WORDS** and purr words point at the intensity of a situation. An argument is different from a fight. The terms were coined by "S.I. Hayakawa" who was a professor of general semantics in US.

## WAS THE FIRST OXFORD DICTIONARY BIASED AGAINST AFRICANS?

🎓 **THE FACT THAT** the word "African" was omitted from the first edition of the Oxford English Dictionary while the word "American" made it to the printing press would give rise to such doubts. Moreover, many believed that the first edition of the Oxford Dictionary, which was published in 1884, primarily catered to Victorian gentlemen, so would naturally be biased against Africans.

But a twist in the tale suggests that it wasn't really so. Bias didn't really play a role in "African" getting omitted from the first edition of the dictionary. Initially, the dictionary's editor James Murray was against including any proper nouns in the dictionary. So the word "African" was dropped. Later on, the rule was changed. But the book had already moved past "African" and reached "American," the latter was thus allowed to stay.

A corrected re-issue of the dictionary was published in 1933.

### 461 FAST FACT...

📖 **WORDS THAT** do not make it into the Oxford English Dictionary are stored in a vault.

### 462 FAST FACT...

📖 **IN 1921,** Czech playwright Karel Capek named the artificial people as "robot" in his play "Rossum's Universal Robots" after the Czech word "robota," which meant forced labor. That's how the word "robot" got coined.

### 463 FAST FACT...

📖 **GOBBLEDYGOOK** stands for jargons. It was first used by US Representative Maury Maverick in 1944.

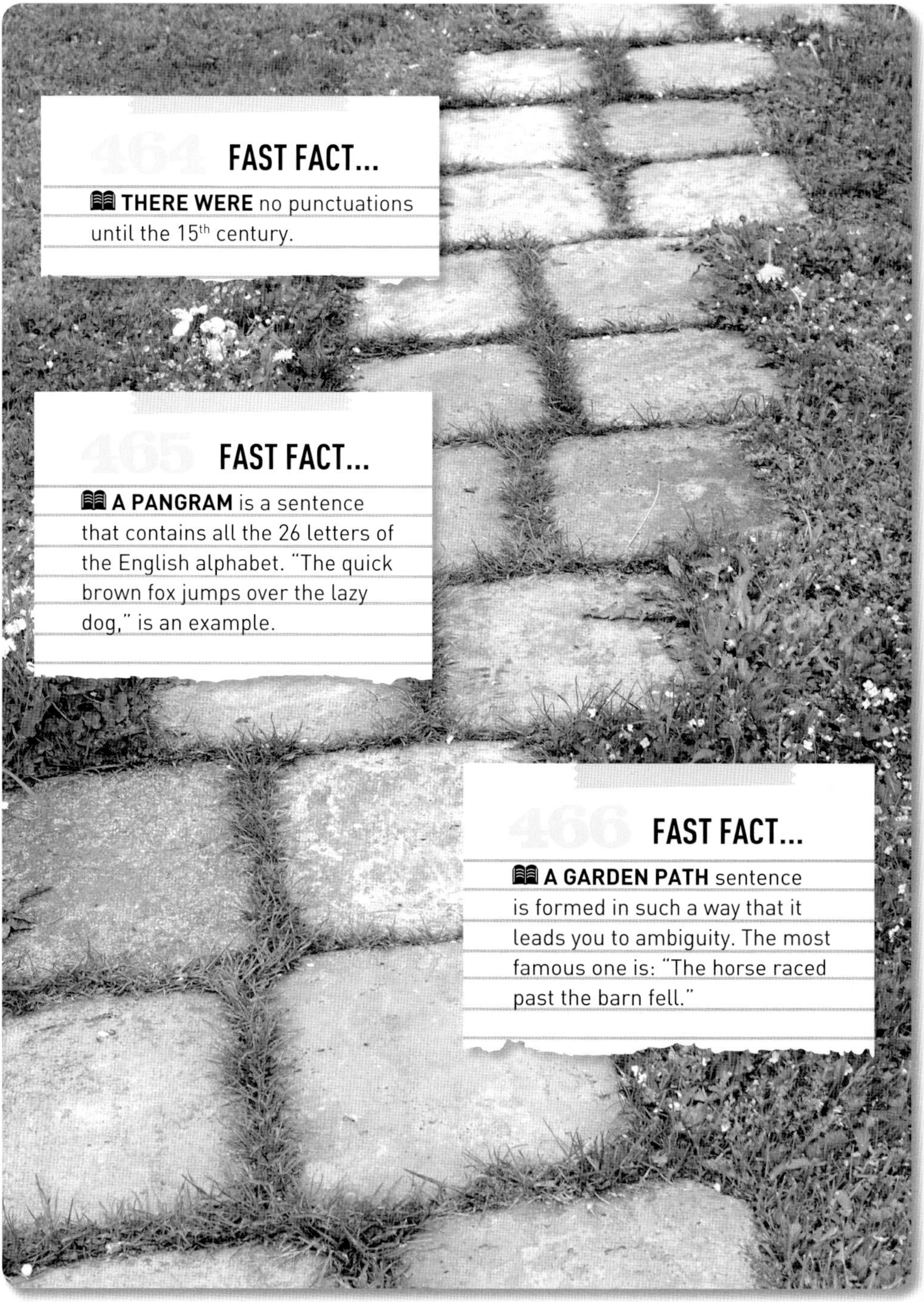

## FAST FACT...

**464**

📖 **THERE WERE** no punctuations until the 15th century.

## FAST FACT...

**465**

📖 **A PANGRAM** is a sentence that contains all the 26 letters of the English alphabet. "The quick brown fox jumps over the lazy dog," is an example.

## FAST FACT...

**466**

📖 **A GARDEN PATH** sentence is formed in such a way that it leads you to ambiguity. The most famous one is: "The horse raced past the barn fell."

# WHERE DID CRASH BLOSSOM COME FROM?

**CRASH BLOSSOM** is a kind of garden path sentence that makes its way to the headlines. Imagine the confusion those bold, black letters would cause! While we sympathize with the readers battling such crash blossoms, we also wonder where the term came from.

Here's the answer to that one. The words "Crash Blossom" were first used in the online edition of Japan Today in the headline: VIOLONIST LINKED TO JAL CRASH BLOSSOMS. The report was about an emerging musician whose father was killed in a famous plane crash. But now her career was blossoming!

Soon, the term "crash blossoms" was picked up by alert copy editors and used on a site. That's how the name was stuck.

## FAST FACT...

**"TELL ME AND** I forget, teach me and I remember, involve me and I learn." – Benjamin Franklin.

## FAST FACT...

**"RULES MUST** be binding. Violations must be punished. Words must mean something." – Barrack Obama.

## HILLARY CLINTON USED A GOOD CHIASMUS

🎓 **WHAT HILLARY CLINTON** said on March 2008, "In the end, the true test is not the speeches a president delivers; it's whether the president delivers on the speeches," was a perfect example of a "chiasmus."

For all the lost souls, chiasmus is the tweaking a sentence by shuffling its words in such a way that you get a witty output. The second half of the sentence is usually the shuffled first half.

The word "chiasmus" originated in 1871 from the Latin word "khiasmos" which meant "a placing crosswise, diagonal arrangement."

### FAST FACT...

📖 **MONOLOGOPHOBIA** is the fear of repeating a word in the sentence. Know someone who suffers from it?

### FAST FACT...

📖 **"PROPER WORDS** in proper places make the true definition of style." – Jonathan Swift.

Johnathan Swift

## TRY THE TRICOLON

· · · · · · · · · · · · · · · · · · · · · · · · · · · · · · · · · · · · · · · · · · · · ·

**IF PUBLIC SPEAKING** is your dream, here's a smart tip on syntax that will really get you places. Of course, it's not one of those well-kept secrets that we're about to reveal. It's just that no one's told you – this is it!

So, this is what it is – a tricolon, a very powerful tool in public speaking that is utilized to its optimum by great orators like Barrack Obama, Abraham Lincoln, Benjamin Franklin, Winston Churchill...the list is long.

A tricolon is a sentence that employs three parts of equal lengths to make their speech sound engaging. For e.g., "We came, we saw, we conquered."

If you're eyeing a standing ovation the next time you stand on a podium, employ a tricolon.

### FAST FACT...

**"I AM NOT** yet so lost in lexicography as to forget that words are the daughters of earth, and that things are the sons of heaven." – Samuel Johnson.

Benjamin Franklin

# TO PAUSE, BUT FOR HOW LONG?

**🎓 OUR SCHOOL TEACHERS FUMED AND FRETTED** over the misplacement of punctuations. Commas, periods, semicolons, and colons all got hopelessly confused when on paper. Why did we get so confused? One prime reason for this could be because we didn't know which pause required what punctuation.

John Mason in "An Essay Of Elocution" (1748) attempted to detangle our misery. "A Comma stops the voice while we may privately tell one, a Semicolon two; a Colon three; and a Period four," he wrote. It paved the way for the syntactic approach that we follow to this date.

When in doubt, read out loud. Gauge for how long it would be apt for the reader to pause. Choose your punctuation accordingly.

## FAST FACT

**📖 APOSTROPHES ARE SUCH** confusing little marks, aren't they? And we aren't the only ones who hate them. Peter Brodie, an English geologist, believed that apostrophes are "largely decorative and rarely clarify meaning." He called them "uncouth bacilli."

## 477 WHY WERE PUNCTUATIONS INVENTED?

**IN ANCIENT GREEK AND ROME,** orators got their speeches prepared in writing. To mark the places where they were supposed to pause, punctuations were invented. But the standardization of punctuations began only once printing came into practice in 1437, thanks to Johann Gutenburg. The process of standardization neared its conclusion by the late 1600s and early 1700s.

Even then, there was a lot of confusion over these tiny marks strewn all over the place. Writers like Chaucer used punctuations as and when they liked.

The punctuations that were used in the first printed books in English were the stroke (/), the colon (: ), and the period (.). In the 16th century, the stroke got replaced by the comma (,). But there was still a long time before the use of punctuations could be standardized.

Author GV Carey observed that "punctuation is governed two-thirds by rule, and one-thirds by personal taste."

## FAST FACT

📖 **SILENT LETTERS IN**
English arise from the fact that although the pronunciation of words has changed over the years, the spelling remains the same.

## FAST FACT

📖 **"CLIMB" IN** Old English was "climban," and "bomb" was "bomba." The sound of b began fading since the 1300s.

## FAST FACT

📖 **"WHAT" HAD A MORE**
phonetically correct spelling as "wot" in the mid-20$^{th}$ century.

## FAST FACT

📖 **AN APRON WAS INITIALLY**
a napron. Yes, the word was napron. However, it always sounded like an apron, which is how napron became redundant.

## 482 UM?

**WHAT'S UM? AS OUR LANGUAGE STEERS** towards the informal terrain, words such as this one pop up. You must have come across at least a handful of "ums" till now. What do they actually mean? Do you think they denote nervousness? Or hesitation, perhaps?

### 483 FAST FACT

**WHILE IT'S "UM" IN** English, it's "euh" in French, "eum" in Korean, and "eh" in Russian.

It's easy to interpret it that way if we're talking about speech. Too many "ums" and you begin to wonder if the speaker is well-prepared. Even there, linguists who love getting at the bottom of everything – even ums – believe that "um" isn't an expression of nervousness. It's a pause impregnated with meaning.

But it's true. An "um" pops up when you can't find the right word, or want to draw attention to a deliberate mistake. It's all a part of style. It's the way you make a listener or reader feel that your point is important enough to ponder. And that ponder is denoted with an um. Got it?

### 484 FAST FACT

**OOGLY-BOOGLY,** a funny reduplicated word refers to a thing or creature that's so ugly that it scares you.

### 485 FAST FACT

**ORANGE, PURPLE,** silver or month don't rhyme with any other word. So sad!

# WHY DO GREETINGS USUALLY BEGIN WITH AN H?

**HI, HEYA, AND HELLO ALL BEGIN FROM H.** Ever noticed? Once we did, we set out to find out why it is so. It seems that the Anglo-Saxons are to be blamed for this one too. They used the h-word to grab attention. While hey and ho date back to the 13th century, hi is the produce of the 15th century. And all this happened because "hal" for Anglo Saxons meant "being healthy." Expressions of greetings began with "be healthy" in those times. Sweet.

It was in the 18th century that "hello" started gaining formal importance. This was mostly because of the invention of the telephone.

## FAST FACT

**THE SOUND OF "AH"** gradually gave way to "oh" by the end of the Anglo-Saxon era. It played a major role in the evolution of the word "loaf" from "hlaf."

## FAST FACT

**JUST LIKE** the smallest unit of matter is the atom in science, the smallest unit in language is called a morpheme, which denotes the smallest unit of meaning.

## FAST FACT

**SHAKESPEARE CREATED** the "un-" prefix, and invented words like unaware, uncomfortable, undress, etc.

## 490 REDUPLICATION FOLLOWS A PATTERN

🎓 Have you **EVER OBSERVED REDUPLICATED WORDS CLOSELY?** If you make a list of reduplicated words like dilly-dally, riff-raff, ping-pong, etc., you will notice that the vowel in the first word is high up in the mouth while that of the next word is low.

That's usually how these reduplicated words are formed. No one actually sat and studiously designed this rule, but we as a species like to say it that way. It's more easy-breezy. Who would like to replace that with breezy-easy?

## 491 FAST FACT

📖 **WILLIAM SHAKESPEARE** was fond of reduplication. We spot words like skimble-skamble and bibble-babble in his plays. Repetition of similar words with slight variation is called reduplication.

## 492 FAST FACT

📖 **THE PREFIX "MEGA-" BECAME** popular only by the end of the 19th century when it started getting attention from the scientists.

## 493 FAST FACT

📖 **"I DON'T GIVE** a damn for a man that can only spell a word in one way." – Mark Twain.

# HOW UN-IN-ONE-BREATH-UTTERABLE CAME ABOUT?

🎓 **WHILE THE "UN-" PREFIX WAS GIFTED** to the English language by William Shakespeare, the suffix "–able" strolled in from its French origins. Gradually, the word list of English increased as these suffixes and prefixes attached themselves to existing words to form new words like unhappily, unhappiness or doable, manageable, etc.

Ben Johnson, who was a Jacobian poet, essayist, and playwright of the 14th century coined the term "un-in-one-breath-utterable."

## FAST FACT

📖 **IF YOU THOUGHT MUSIC** could be spelt only one way, take a look at this list of spellings to see what the word went through in the past – musiqe, mysyque, musique, musyk, music, musike, musick, musicke.

## FAST FACT

📖 **AN APTRONYM** gets its name from the fact that the name is "apt" for the person it's used for. The term was coined by Franklin P. Adams.

## FAST FACT

📖 **AN EXAMPLE OF** a real life aptronym is Usain Bolt, the Jamaican sprinter, whose speed reminds us of a bolt of lightning.

## 498 CUTTING IT SHORT

**PEOPLE LOVED TO CUT SHORT WORDS,** as suggested by David Crystal in the book "The Story of English in 100 Words." That's what gave rise to short forms after all, right? In the 17th century, when clipping was a rage, the word "reputation" was cut short to "rep." What makes this short form really interesting is the fact that the meaning of "rep" hasn't remained the same since.

Thomas Jefferson

In the 18th century, "rep" stood for the word reprobate, which referred to an immoral person. The word changed meaning yet again after that, and appeared with the capital R to represent Republic. Then, the House of Reps stood for the House of Representatives, and in the 19th century, a member of the Republican party came to be known as a Rep.

It was post the 1930s that reps became short for repetitions and came to be used extensively in gyms; 30-reps, 100-reps, and so on.

## 499 FAST FACT

**"MY NAME IS ONLY** an anagram of toilets." – TS Eliot

## 500 FAST FACT

**"TAKE CARE THAT YOU** never spell a word wrong. Before you write a word, consider how it is spelled, and, if you do not remember, turn to a dictionary. It produces great praise to a lady to spell well." – Thomas Jefferson wrote to his daughter Martha.

## 501 FAST FACT

**AN IRRATIONAL FEAR** of palindromes is called "Aibohphobia." Aibohp is phobia spelled backwards!

# INDEX

## A

accents 100, 104, 108, 113, 115
acronyms 29, 190, 217
adjectives 62, 95, 121, 132, 147, 196, 212, 234
adverbs 121, 135-6, 147, 160, 168
Africans 235
Ælfric 81
alliteration 137-8
American Dictionary 67, 102, 205
Americans 56, 101, 109, 226, 235
Angles 62, 68, 70, 190, 228
Anglo-Saxons 75-6, 106, 222, 228, 244
   Anglo-Saxon words 78
anticlimax 133
apostrophes 183, 229, 240
aptronym 246
archaism 69, 94
   archaic elements 94
ashram 151, 154
assassination 16, 194, 198
Augustan Literature 42-3
Austen, Jane 49-50, 141, 202
Australia 31-2, 45, 214

## B

Beowulf 68, 77, 83
Bible 9, 18, 25, 38, 95, 181, 206
   King James Bible 23, 25-6
   New Bible 25
Blake, William 36, 38

Britain 31, 46, 62, 75-6, 79, 213-14
   East coast of Britain 70, 75
British Colonialism 31

## C

Caesar, Julius 79, 95, 98, 103, 133, 141
Canterbury Tales 69, 92-3
Caroll, Lewis 46, 48
Celtic Mythology 80, 84
Celtic religion 80
century 12-15, 17, 22-4, 29-31, 35-6, 47, 49, 62-3, 65-6, 81-4, 210-11, 216, 221-3, 228-9, 244-7
Chancery English 10
Chaucer, Geoffrey 91-3, 182, 241
chiasmus 238
children 23, 46, 48, 110, 118-19, 138, 142, 166, 182, 213
China 52, 105
Chinese Pidgin English 110
Chomsky 194, 199
Christ 86, 190
Christianity 80, 86
Churchill, Winston 121, 126, 239
classics 10, 40, 45, 103, 107, 202
clauses 133-4
cliché 96, 124
climax 133
Clinton, Hillary 238
Cockney 104-5, 180
colons 240-1

comma  22, 240-1

common howlers  8, 173-4, 183

computers  52, 149, 166, 234

concept  66, 98, 113, 119

confusion  13, 23, 88, 97, 149, 224, 231, 237, 241

conjunctions  134

consonance  137

content  8, 36, 38, 51, 92

countries  45, 50, 75, 140

creoles  110, 112

Cupertino effect  178


## D

Defoe, Daniel  34-5

Di, Charles  53, 55

Dickens, Charles  45-6, 53, 195, 204, 225

dictionary  13, 20, 43, 61, 66, 94, 192, 195, 201, 207, 218, 222, 233, 235, 247

dictionary of English language  201, 205, 213

digraph  87-8, 96

Donne, John  14

Dryden, John  12, 66


## E

EC Booze  216

Edgar Allen Poe  40-1

editing  179

Elizabethan English  98

Emma  50, 202

England  10, 19-20, 25, 27, 33, 36, 43, 62-3, 65-6, 78, 89, 98, 104, 141, 162

English  8, 62, 101, 227-8

English accent  104

English alphabet  163, 165-6, 236

English grammar  8, 9, 13-14, 22, 24, 49, 59, 62-3, 65-6, 70, 82, 93, 95-6, 98, 164

English Literature  25, 50, 103, 107

English phrases  95, 97

English vocabulary  27-9, 77, 212, 216, 219, 225

English words  10, 17, 30, 65, 103, 110, 154, 169

errors  177, 179

grammatical errors  206

Europe  18, 36, 72

European languages  17, 73

evolution  42, 61, 63, 65, 94, 125, 244


## F

feminist literature  51

fiction, fantastic  47

fopdoodle  209, 218

Franklin, Benjamin  204, 237, 239

French, Norman  65, 76


## G

garden path sentence  236-7

Gauls  79-80

gazette  230

Germanic, ancient 62-3, 65, 70, 75
Globish 52
grammar rules 15, 66, 196, 199
grammar teachers 182, 197
grammarians 29, 125, 135, 143-4
grammatical structure 59, 111
Great Vowel Shift 17, 98
Greek 10, 72, 103, 118, 123, 151-2, 154, 216
Greek words 126, 216, 219, 222
Greengrocer's Apostrophe 183
Gulliver 43-4

## H

Hart, John 22
Hawthorne 40-1
headlines 237
Hillebrand 186
Hinglish 52, 111
history 35, 40, 66, 152, 177, 227, 230
Homer 135, 212
Horsa 70-1
Huckleberry Finn 55-6
hyperbole 141, 145

## I

idioms 45, 143, 145
India 31-2, 52, 72, 111
Industrial Revolution 27, 38
interjections 134-5, 212
irony 116, 123

## J

jabberwocky 220, 233
Jefferson, Thomas 247
Johannes Gutenberg 18
Johnson
    Ben 15-16, 246
    Samuel 43, 66, 201, 213, 239
Jones, William 73, 154

## K

Keats, John 38-9
Kempe, Margery 89
kennings 69, 77, 83
King Charles II 226, 230
King Henry VII 25-6, 84
Kipling 194-5, 200

## L

languages 31-3, 62-3, 71-4, 76-7, 79, 89, 94, 97-8, 102, 110-13, 118-20, 132, 152-5, 211, 228
    ancient languages 152
    Celtic languages 79-80
    classical languages 12, 14, 27, 103
    colloquial language 93
    computer language 52
    English language 10, 13-15, 17, 19, 25, 29, 31-2, 64-7, 95, 102-3, 132, 159, 169, 200-1, 204-5
    Foreign language 66, 122
    Global language 52

human languages 112, 125
Indic language and Persian 152
indiscernible languages 32
Indo-European language 73
Italic languages 152
Jane's language 202
Middle English language 93
Native language 25, 112
Official language 111
Old Norse language 78
Programming language 52
proto-Indo-European language 152
Latin 10, 14, 28, 32, 60, 66, 72, 76, 78-9,
    81, 89, 92-3, 97, 103, 154-5
    Latin grammar 66
legal doublets 97
legalese 97
letters 13, 24, 48, 53, 64, 67, 82, 87-8, 92,
    98, 159, 165-7, 169, 187-8, 234
Liberman, Mark 174
linguists 8, 108, 112, 125, 132, 135, 147,
    243
literary field 14
literary works 82, 84
literature 14, 35-6, 40, 42, 46-7, 49, 80,
    86, 89, 98, 122-3, 151, 155
loanwords 32, 79
LOL 184, 188
lyrics 176


## M

malapropism 175-6, 178
Man-Friday 35

Mark Twain 55-6, 123, 132-3, 147, 203,
    245
meh 212
metaphors 46, 83, 117, 124, 129, 145
Middle English 22, 76, 87-9, 92, 95
Milton, John 11, 14, 66
mistake 59, 96, 168, 174, 176, 179, 181,
    203
Modern English 62, 78, 86-9, 92, 95-6, 98,
    160, 168
Mondegreens 176
music 57, 223, 246
mythology 80, 82


## N

napron 242
nature 38-9, 45, 51, 81, 86, 97, 125, 130
negation 136
negative particle 136
newspaper 115, 230
non-Latin characters 88
Norman 76, 88-9, 106
Norse 61, 63, 74, 82
Northern England 75
nouns 22, 62-3, 118-21, 132, 135, 139-40,
    145, 149, 170, 196, 235
    common nouns 119, 196
novels 34, 36, 42, 45-6, 48, 53, 55-6
number, grammatical 132

# O

Old English  62, 65, 75-8, 81-3, 86-7, 89,
  152, 242
Old Norse  75-6, 82
onomatopoeia  125
Oxford Dictionary  87-8, 94, 160, 168, 235
oxymoron  126

# P

pangram  157, 166, 236
passive voice  59
past tense forms  169
pause  240-1, 243
pen names  55
personification  130-1
philosophy  42, 151, 155, 177
phonograph  57-8
phrases  15, 44-6, 97, 104, 110, 121-2,
  133-4, 137, 143, 145, 226, 229, 232
pidgins  110, 112
plural  62, 103, 119, 126, 132, 148, 183,
  229, 231
poems  15, 20, 40, 53, 77, 83, 86, 90-1,
  138, 148, 233
  famous poems  86, 90, 130
poetry  36, 38, 40, 42-3, 46, 48, 57, 83, 86,
  94, 122, 137, 223
poets  43, 91, 93, 130, 160
Pope, Alexander  44
portmanteau  220
prefixes  28, 76, 95, 103, 244-6
prepositions  12, 66, 116, 121-2
prescriptions  217

printing  19, 96, 241
printing press  18-21, 235
pronouns  23, 62-3, 75, 96, 108, 112, 121,
  136
  male  24
  person pronouns  106, 139
  personal pronouns  21, 139
  plural pronouns  112
  third person plural pronouns  63
pronunciations  17, 57, 75, 88, 108, 148,
  161, 216, 228, 242
proofreading  179
proverbs  43, 145-6
punctuations  22, 236, 240-1
puns  98, 117, 127-8, 147

# Q

Queen's English  101, 104, 113, 115
QWERTY  234

# R

Rebus  184, 187
repetition  137, 245, 247
revelation  182, 188, 234
rhymes  98, 104-5, 180, 243
Robinson Crusoe  33-5
Romantic Era  36, 38
Romanticism  36, 38-9
  American Romanticism  40
Romantic Movement  36, 38
Rudyard Kipling  200, 230

# S

Sanskrit  72, 152, 154-5

Sanskrit and English Grammar  8, 151

satire  42-3

Saxons  62, 68, 70, 84, 228

scholars  10, 12-13, 26-7, 29, 72, 110, 112, 124, 152, 154

Scottish dictionary  220

self-explaining compounds  28

semicolons  240

sentences  22, 62-3, 65-6, 87, 121, 133-5, 143-4, 147, 166, 168, 170-1, 182, 186-7, 199, 238-9

Shakespeare  15-16, 22-3, 66, 69, 95, 98, 182, 193-4, 196-8, 244-6

silent letters  9, 12-13, 205

similes  117, 129, 145

slang  180, 221, 231

SMS  184-5, 190-1, 193

sonnets  15-16

speakers  104, 106, 110, 112-13, 152, 229, 243

speech  8, 57, 94, 106, 108, 117, 120, 123-6, 129, 133, 135, 137, 145, 170, 238

spellings  12-13, 17, 21-2, 67, 100, 102, 125, 148, 195, 202, 210, 225, 228, 231, 242

Spooner  172-3, 177

stalwarts  8, 60, 195, 197

story  30, 34-5, 38, 42, 48, 84, 89, 91-2, 148, 174, 176-7, 186, 211, 220, 229-31

subjects  36, 43, 53, 89, 103, 106, 118, 147, 152

suffixes  28, 75-6, 95, 103, 111, 119, 132, 136, 246

Suffrage Movement  49-50

Swift, Jonathan  42-3, 128, 222, 225, 238

symbols  190, 217

syntax  62, 65, 199, 239

# T

telegraph  57

telephone  57, 103-4, 244

tricolon  239

tweeps  192

# U

USA  229, 231

usage  22, 96-7, 115, 118, 139, 158, 182, 216, 225, 229

correct usage  168

# V

verbs  30, 62-3, 95, 116, 118, 121, 132, 135, 147-8, 154, 168, 196

irregular verbs  118

phrasal verbs  121

verb form  161, 170

Victorian Era  45-8, 84, 221

Vikings  63, 68, 74-6, 78

vocabulary  10, 14, 75, 96, 113, 152, 192, 197, 199

vowel sounds  137, 139

vowels  9, 17, 20, 104, 107, 149, 245

## W

Walt Whitman  40-1
Watt, James  9, 27
Webster  13, 195, 206
  Noah  32-3, 67, 102, 205-7
Welsh  90
West Germanic  62, 70, 78
Wordsworth, William  37-8

## Y

Ye Olde English  96
yoghurt  67
Yorkshire dialect  106